Mr. Justice Jackson

FOUR
LECTURES
IN HIS
HONOR

Mr. Justice Jackson

FOUR
LECTURES
IN HIS
HONOR
BY

CHARLES S. DESMOND, PAUL A. FREUND,

POTTER STEWART, AND LORD SHAWCROSS

Delivered under the Auspices of
The Association of the Bar of the City of New York and
The William Nelson Cromwell Foundation

Published as one of the Legal Studies
of The William Nelson Cromwell Foundation
by Columbia University Press
New York and London
1969

Copyright © 1969 Columbia University Press
Library of Congress Catalog Card Number: 78-89566
Printed in the United States of America

TRUSTEES

OF

THE WILLIAM NELSON CROMWELL FOUNDATION

Contents

General Introduction by Whitney North Seymour,
Esq.   1

The Role of the Country Lawyer in the Organized
Bar and the Development of the Law, by The
Honorable Charles S. Desmond, with an Intro-
duction by John Lord O'Brian, Esq.   7

Mr. Justice Jackson and Individual Rights, by Professor Paul A. Freund, with an Introduction by
The Honorable Charles D. Breitel   29

Robert H. Jackson's Influence on Federal-State Relationships, by The Honorable Potter Stewart,
with an Introduction by The Honorable John
M. Harlan   57

Robert H. Jackson's Contributions During the Nur-
emberg Trial, by The Right Honorable Lord
Shawcross, with an Introduction by Whitney
North Seymour, Esq.   87

Mr. Justice Jackson

FOUR
LECTURES
IN HIS
HONOR

General Introduction

WHITNEY NORTH SEYMOUR, ESQ.

Mr. Justice Robert H. Jackson died at the age of 62 on October 9, at the beginning of the 1954 Term of the Supreme Court. His heart had warned him before that his burdens were too heavy, but his courageous nature and sense of duty did not admit slippered ease as a tolerable alternative. Death thus ended the extraordinarily varied public career of one who took pride in having been a country lawyer from Jamestown, New York, whose formal academic career ended with high school and one year at Albany Law School, but whose insatiable curiosity led him to master history and politics as well as law. Admitted to the New York Bar in 1913, he engaged in a comprehensive law practice in Jamestown for twenty years, during which he became one of the leading trial lawyers of upstate New York. Restless for a part in the excitement of the early days of the New Deal, he was induced by President Roosevelt to come to Washington in 1934 as General Counsel to the Bureau of Internal Revenue in the Treasury Department. It was typical of his independence that he consulted his two old friends, Judge Sears and John Lord O'Brian, about this, and when they advised him to hold out for something of broader scope, he rejected their advice and twitted them afterward about their lack of vision. They could hardly have foreseen how fast he would rise from this rather unpromising beginning. In one of the fastest progressions in legal history, within seven years thereafter he became successively Assistant Attorney General in charge of the Tax Division, Chief of the Antitrust Division, followed the Hon. Stanley Reed as Solicitor General, then followed the Hon. Frank Murphy as Attorney General. Finally, in 1941, at the age of 49, he was appointed to the Supreme Court as an Associate Justice, filling the vacancy created when President Roosevelt appointed Mr. Justice Stone as Chief Justice.

His service on the Supreme Court produced many notable opinions, written in a spare, pithy style, completely individual and setting forth the problem and its solution in an unforgettable way. Readers of the opinions of the Court could always spot a Jackson opinion by its characteristic liveliness and practical good sense. As references to some of the opinions in these lectures show, few Justices in the history of the Court have written in a clearer or more sparkling style. Indeed, sparkle is a rather unusual ingredient in Supreme Court opinions. In the middle of his service on the Court he was drafted by President Truman to negotiate the final arrangements for trial of the Nazi war criminals and then to present the American case against them before the Nuremberg Tribunal, a service of which he and most other Americans were very proud, because it helped to vindicate international law and give new content to the rule of law.

Both as lawyer and judge he cherished and contributed to the brotherhood of the bar. Charming, companionable, unpretentious, gay, and humorous, he loved being with lawyers and they with him. A founder of the Federation of Bar Associations of Western New York, he was active in the New York and American Bar Associations. He was in constant demand as a speaker at Bar Associations and for those equally important convivial gatherings of lawyers which always follow speeches.

It was inevitable that such a person would be loved and admired by his colleagues and that he would have a vast circle of friends including his seniors, juniors, and contemporaries. In his time, he was certainly the most effective catalytic agent between Bench and Bar. Some years after his death, the void which he left naturally led to the suggestion that it should be filled, in part, by a series of memorial lectures which would refresh recollections of those who had known him and also remind a new generation about his personal, professional, and judicial qualities. The inspired trio of friends who conceived the plan were Mr. Justice Frankfurter, long his colleague on the Court and close friend, Mr. Justice Harlan, who succeeded him on the Supreme Court and as the greatly admired Circuit Justice of the Second Circuit (and who, like him, is regarded everywhere as the model of a lawyer's judge), and John Lord O'Brian, Esq., the dean of the American Bar who, like Jackson, was a gift to the nation from western New York. They found allies in E. Barrett Prettyman, Jr. and the other young men who had the privilege of being Jackson law clerks.

The Association of the Bar, with the approval of Presidents Rosenman and Niles and of Paul B. De Witt, its talented Executive Secretary, and under the auspices of the Committee on Post-Admission Legal Education, of which E. Nobles Lowe was the imaginative Chairman, undertook to include the lectures as part of its program. The William Nelson Cromwell Foundation cooperated in arranging for the lectures and this publication.

We were extraordinarily fortunate in the choice of lecturers and those who introduced them. Although each of the four lectures deals with a particular facet of the Jackson career, they cover main segments and illumine both his personal and professional qualities. No doubt, in due time, all will be pulled together in a definitive biography. Meantime, these are worthy of the subject and the reader will rise from them with fresh insights about Jackson and his extraordinary qualities of mind and heart.

Former Chief Judge Charles S. Desmond of the New York Court of Appeals, himself from the same part of upstate New York as Jackson, deals in the first lecture with Jackson as a country lawyer. We were fortunate indeed to have John Lord O'Brian introduce Judge Desmond and give his own appraisal of Jackson's personality and qualities, based upon a long and affectionate friendship. His emphasis on personality as a key quality in great people is a refreshing part of his remarks.

Professor Paul A. Freund of Harvard Law School, a student without peer of the Supreme Court and the Constitution, Editor-in-Chief of the History of the Supreme Court under the Holmes Devise, and a colleague of Jackson's as Solicitor General, out of his own affection for Jackson and for Frankfurter, in the second lecture deals with the great Jackson opinions in the field of personal liberty. Judge Charles D. Breitel, a scholarly and perceptive member of the Court of Appeals and, himself, a student of Jackson's work, gives a notable introduction to Professor Freund. The third lecture provides, in effect, participation by two of the leading present members of the Supreme Court. Mr.

Justice Stewart offers the lecture dealing primarily with Jackson's contributions on the Court to concepts of Federal State relationships. Mr. Justice Harlan contributes a notable introduction. The final lecture deals appropriately with Jackson's role at Nuremberg, which he regarded as probably the major contribution of his life. For this lecture we had the good fortune of having the Rt. Hon. Lord Shawcross, who had a hand in arranging for the structure of Nuremberg and, as British Attorney General, had official responsibility for the English presentation, much of which was carried on by his predecessor as Attorney General, another great friend of the American Bar, Sir David Maxwell Fyfe (later Earl Kilmuir). Lord Shawcross had been enterprising enough to procure tapes of some of Jackson's speeches at Nuremberg and interpolated them into his address.

For those who knew Robert Jackson these lectures and their introductions conjure him up so that one can almost see him reading an opinion on the Court or addressing a Bar Association or exchanging anecdotes in an intimate circle. For those who did not have the privilege of knowing him, it is hoped that these lectures will help to insure that his contributions, career, and spirit will remain a part of the tradition of comradeship of Bench and Bar and of the great concepts of equal justice for all and of the rule of law which were part of his dream, as they are of ours.

We are grateful to William E. Jackson, Esq., of the New York Bar, the Justice's son, now one of our leading trial lawyers and his aide at Nuremberg, for assisting in the preparation of this volume. Henry N. Ess, III, Esq., the Cromwell Foundation's Secretary-Treasurer, assisted in working out arrangements for the lectures and has been an effective liaison between the Foundation and the publisher.

The Role of the Country Lawyer
in the Organized Bar
and the Development of the Law

THE HONORABLE CHARLES S. DESMOND
With an Introduction by
JOHN LORD O'BRIAN, ESQ.

As one of those who were interested in arranging these lectures, I feel very grateful that you have come out this evening to listen to a tribute on the part of the main speaker to a man for whom I had infinite admiration and affection.

When, many years ago, I moved Robert Jackson's admission to the Supreme Court, I had no idea that I was moving the admission of a future member of that Court, and neither did he. I would like to contribute a few words on my own account about him, not about his work, that will be dealt with adequately elsewhere but something about the personality of the man himself.

After a reasonably long life, and I am only ninety-two, about the age when Holmes retired, I have realized more and more what the factor of personality means in public life, in providing a man with the gift of influence. That elusive element, which I think you will agree is so often

missed by biographers and historians, is to me a very important element in the evolution of Robert Jackson.

He grew up as a farm boy in northwestern Pennsylvania
on a farm where his ancestors had lived for three generations. His formal education ended in high school. He was
interested in law and he went to work in the local law office
of a relative. After a few years he borrowed some money
and went to the Albany Law School for one year, not for
the full term.

That was the extent of his formal legal education and
those are the facts which give such singularity to his career
in American public life. But entirely apart from the great
ability that he very early showed and which increased with
the years, there was another element, and that was his personality.

He grew up in a community of very ordinary people, but
he was different. He had ambition and he had some rare
qualities of character that were not immediately apparent,
but which emerged with the years. His success as a great
lawyer and a great judge came, I think, not only from his
unusual ability as a lawyer, but also from the character of
his own personality and the great charm which he exercised
over everybody with whom he came in contact. He was a
man of very profound and strong convictions, but he was
born to be a good-natured man. He never yielded his convictions, but in his personal association he was singularly
tolerant of the views of other people.

In his style, as those who are familiar with his work
know, he developed a richness that at times seemed almost
inconsistent with the clarity and the lucidity with which he
wrote and spoke. That lucidity came, I have always
thought, from the fact that as a trial lawyer in local courts

he had such difficulty in making clear the legal issues in cases that were before the court. Out of that came a very remarkable development on his part; for, from the beginning of his career as a lawyer to the end, he was noted for his clarity, his lucidity, and his directness. He rarely used metaphors, or figures of speech, and yet the law professors tell us today that, aside from Cardozo, no one on the Supreme Court developed a richer, more meaningful English style than he did. As I have heard Justice Cardozo say, what first attracted him to Jackson in his arguments before the Court of Appeals was the extraordinary quality of freshness and directness of approach. He was singularly observant by nature. Very early in life, because of his contact with many ordinary people, he came to have an uncanny understanding of the motivations that inflenced the lives of ordinarily plain men and women, and I think that was one of his greatest gifts.

He was not interested in speculative philosophy. In fact he humorously said once that people among whom he grew up were too busy earning a living to put or to try to coordinate the annoyances of life into a system of philosophy. That was quite characteristic of the man himself. I think, if he had heard it, he would have agreed with that friend of Dr. Samuel Johnson, Mr. Edwards, who said to Dr. Johnson, "You know, I have tried very hard to be a philosopher, but somehow or another—I don't know the reason— cheerfulness always breaks in." I think that Bob Jackson would have sympathized with that view.

The key to his whole career might be found in a single illustration of his independence. During the First World War, although many have forgotten it, we were subjected to the same climate of hysteria and emotional excitement that existed in the Second World War, and I suppose always will in times of emergency. In Jamestown, the workers on the traction line went on strike. To say that it was an unpopular strike would be an understatement, because of the discomfort caused to the patrons of the traction company. The workers were thereupon indicted for a violation of the laws which were generally grouped under the head of syndicalism—which we would say was communism.

Jackson was outraged by this indictment. He had not yet been admitted to the bar, but nobody else appearing, he promptly came forward and volunteered his services to defend these unpopular strikers. With the permission of the Court, because he had not yet been admitted to the bar, he was permitted to act as their defense counsel and secured their acquittal.

That produced for the time being an outraged feeling on the part of the general community, who dubbed him as a radical and a syndicalist, a communist. It made no difference to him. That first act of courageous, independent conduct, based on his conscientious conviction, was typical of his entire career.

In another respect, even from boyhood, he was marked out separately. He was always a person of very independent character. Though he was very tolerant of other people's views, at least he listened to them patiently, he never changed his own fundamental convictions unless under the persuasion of his conscience. One of his favorite quotations was a line from Kipling: "He travels farthest who travels alone." That doesn't mean that he was what is in the parlance of today called a loner, but it does mean that he was independent in all of his personal convictions and his personal acts; and although this may seem singular to us, he was never a member of any political organization. He was very active politically in later life, but he never consented to be a member or committed to the organization of any party or any other type of organization. The nearest he ever came to that was as a vestryman of the Episcopal church in his community. That, so far as I know, was the only affiliation he ever made.

Another instance of his remarkable courage came fairly early in his career, after he was better known at the bar. In the governorship of Franklin Roosevelt, the Legislature provided for the appointment of a commission to make a study of crime in New York state. Some of the men were selected by the Bar Association, some by the Legislature, and some by the Governor.

Governor Roosevelt, exercising the authority given him, made a decision as to who should be chairman of this commission. Word was brought to him that Jackson, who had been nominated by the Bar Association, announced he would not vote for that selection. The Governor sent for him, and I need not say that Mr. Roosevelt was a man of strong views. Jackson took the position that he was not interested in the personality of the chairman, but he objected to anyone being appointed chairman who was not a person who had wide experience in the administration of the criminal law. He said he would not vote for a man to be chairman of this commission who simply had an academic background.

They had quite an argument. It came to no conclusion, apparently, and they separated. A week later, Franklin Roosevelt appointed a man Jackson had mentioned to be chairman of the commission.

That was only one example of his independence and his

courage. *There is another little-known episode. When Frank Murphy was elevated from the office of the Attorney General to be a member of the Supreme Court, Jackson was at that time Solicitor General of the United States, a position which appealed to him more than any other of his whole life. Word came, or word was passed, as we say in Washington, that Jackson would be selected as the next Attorney General.*

Jackson sat down and wrote a long letter addressed to the President, saying he had heard these rumors and he certainly appreciated the compliment that was implied; but he was not in sympathy with certain policies of his predecessor which he described and defined. He thought he ought not to be appointed Attorney General because he wished to say right now that if he were appointed he would not pursue any of those policies. President Roosevelt never answered that letter, but to his credit, a week later he appointed Jackson Attorney General of the United States.

I think that is one of the most remarkable instances of frankness that I know. I don't use the word candor any more. I would have used that in connection with Jackson because his frankness and sense of fair play were two of the most conspicuous characteristics of his efficacy in argument. But one day, in talking with the late Justice Holmes, I unfortunately remarked that I had been impressed with what one of the opinions of the court had said about the candor of the Attorney General, William Mitchell. The old man, looking at me with that skeptical and penetrating eye, said, "Candor, yes, that is a word that I don't use because I have found that candor judiciously applied is one of the most dangerous methods of deception."

Since then, I too have abandoned the use of that word,

but I would like to say something about Jackson's friendships, of which I fortunately know a good deal.

Felix Frankfurter, says that the ultimate test of greatness in a man is his capacity for gratitude. Jackson had that in a supreme degree. He was devoted to his friends. He never failed to remind them of a sense of obligation that he felt toward their friendship. The one person who most affected his early life was a school teacher in Jamestown who, so to speak, spotted this boy as unusual, took him under her wing, and aroused his interest in literature and music. He never failed, when an opportunity came up, to mention that woman by name, and tell how she had helped him. This was true of all of his friendships. He had a nostalgic feeling for early friends, and went out of his way to remind them of it, even though he might not see them for long intervals.

One other thing I would like to mention, and that is his humor. He was not given to anecdotal humor or smart aleck phrases, or telling stories. But he was gifted with that old Elizabethan folk humor in the true sense. Keenly observant all his life, he quickly recognized the amusing incongruities of daily life, not only everyday life, but life among men whom we call statesmen. When he was offered the position of General Counsel for the Internal Revenue Bureau at the outset of the Roosevelt administration, he talked with several of his friends. Two of the men that he consulted with were men who were his old friends, the late Justice Sears and myself. We very emphatically urged him not to take that post, but to wait for a post that was more worthy of his gifts and where he would have a greater opportunity for influencing the course of the law and the course of procedure. He paid no attention to us. He never failed later in life, to ridicule us as false prophets and to make fun of us as advisers, as shortsighted and incapable men who didn't understand the world, because in seven years after he accepted that post he became an Associate Justice of the Supreme Court of the United States.

He was a man of great innate dignity, something far removed from pomposity. But he never cheapened himself to secure anybody's approval. This was a very noble characteristic and he very rarely indulged in comments about his court. I remember one occasion when I was present in the Supreme Court. There is a clock in front and another clock in the rear. The advocate was closing his argument and he turned and looked at both clocks, saying to the court, "May I ask how much time I have left? The clocks do not seem to agree." And Jackson said, "Well, possibly, that is the influence of the atmosphere of the Court."

Those comments were very rare, but on one occasion he quite excelled himself. There was an organization in Washington, called the Alfalfa Club. It has no constitution and no bylaws, and no purpose so far as any can be determined. It simply exists. The club has a dinner every year and one of their customs is to equate themselves into a national convention and nominate a man for president. On this occasion, within ten days after the beginning of the Eisenhower administration, Justice Jackson was the candidate nominated. Jackson delivered a very humorous speech, and no one was more surprised than his old friends. Down to this present day, that speech is quoted and remembered as the most humorous and successful speech ever made in the club's fifty years of existence. In the course of that speech he made one jocular remark that led to some misunderstanding. Referring to the Revised Standard Edition of the Bible, he said that the methods followed by the revisers were not those customary in the Supreme Court because, he said, the revisers of the Bible, in order to make the meaning more clear, had changed the words, whereas, he said, in our court "we keep the words but change the meaning." Fortunately, or unfortunately, I am told that some of those present didn't realize that it was intended as a witticism and solemnly voiced their disagreement with his remark.

But that was Justice Jackson, his simple, straightforward personality as I saw it. It colored all of his work. It colored his advocacy. When he spoke, he had a certain gift of directness, of freshness in approaching a topic without any resort to philosophical soliloquies. That is what endeared him to courts and judges wherever he appeared, and that is what worried his opponents.

He was a very human individual and I say this simply because I have seen so often in the biographies careful records of what a man said and did, accurate in all respects, but still not disclosing the ultimate character of the man himself. I would leave the impression of a very human man, with broad sympathy and profound conviction and devotion to the ultimate tenets of American democracy.

I now introduce former Chief Judge Charles Desmond, who has many qualities which identify him with those of Robert Jackson.

His forthrightness, his basic common sense, is practical empirical view of the law, have marked him quite apart, and we are very grateful that in this day and generation we have not only in our midst a great judge, but also a man who is profoundly interested in the work that the ordinary lawyer seems to feel is distasteful, the work of improving the procedure of the law in this state.

I belong to the tradition of Brandeis and Frankfurter.

Following their example, I firmly believe that one of the most important phases in the development of law before us is not substantive law alone, but procedural law. These are the reforms in procedure that we will continue to seek to bring about a greater recognition of fair play in the administration of the law, particularly in view of all the law that has been created by the administrators.

In addition to these qualities, however, he has another quality that he shares with Justice Jackson. This is his friendliness, his gift of toleration, and his sympathetic attitude in listening to arguments. I think that this is one of the greatest tributes one can pay to any judge, and if you knew of his position in the City of Buffalo you would realize that there he is not only regarded with respect as a judge, but he is regarded with great respect and great affection as a citizen who from the time he came to the bar has actively interested himself in all the good causes of the community. Today there is no one in public life for whom we feel a greater sense of admiration and personal affection than former Chief Judge Charles Desmond.

JOHN LORD O'BRIAN, ESQ.

When Robert Houghwout Jackson described himself as a "country lawyer," he was not simulating humility, boasting of humble origin, or indulging in nostalgic recollections. He was appreciating, perhaps idealizing a bit, what he described as "the county-seat lawyer, counselor to railroads and to Negroes, to bankers and to poor whites, who always gave to each the best that was in him—and was willing to admit that his best was good." Robert Jackson, who sat in the seats of the mighty, who reached the heights of professional glory, was all his life convinced, as he wrote in the little piece I have quoted from that remarkable collection published twenty years ago as "The Practical Cogitator," that the "experience" which gave life to our law (Holmes) was a type of country life from which in the last century came our lawyers, judges, and legislators. Jackson recalled for us that their way of living "generated independence and amazing energy," and that they themselves went to the cities and dominated the professions as well as business, controlled the county courthouses and the state houses, weighing legal doctrines, political theories, and social policies "in the light of the life they knew." Lamenting the disappearance of this "country lawyer" type, Jackson described him thus (and I give you this quotation for the perfection of its portraiture and without apology for its length):

He did not specialize, nor did he pick and choose clients. He rarely declined service to worthy ones because of inability to pay. Once enlisted for a client, he took his obligation seriously. He insisted on complete control of the litigation—he was no mere hired hand. But he gave every power and resource to the cause. He identified himself with the client's cause fully, sometimes too fully. He would fight the adverse party and fight his counsel, fight every hostile witness, and fight the court, fight public sentiment, fight any obstacle to his client's success. He never quit. He could think of motions for every purpose under the sun, and he made them all. He moved for new trials, he appealed; and if he lost out in the end, he joined the client at the tavern in damning the judge—which is the last rite in closing an unsuccessful case, and I have officiated at many. But he loved his profession, he had a real sense of dedication to the administration of justice, he held his head high as a lawyer, he rendered and exacted courtesy, honor, and straightforwardness at the bar. He respected the judicial office deeply, demanded the highest standards of competence and disinterestedness and dignity, despised all political use of or trifling with judicial power, and had an affectionate regard for every man who filled his exacting prescription of the just judge. The law to him was like a religion, and its practice was more than a means of support; it was a mission. He was not always popular in his community, but he was respected. Unpopular minorities and individuals often found in him their only mediator and advocate.

I am sure that Robert Jackson, when he wrote that tribute to a vanishing tribe, was unaware that he was in part describing himself as he practised law in Jamestown, New York, and as he was in spirit and ideal and motivation all the days of his life. The virtue of independence which he praised in others was conspicuously his own, as witnessed by an editorial which appeared in his hometown newspaper in March 1934 when he was appointed and confirmed as General Counsel to the Internal Revenue Bureau. A Senator, opposing confirmation, had suggested that the then Secretary of the Treasury was seeking "yes men" (including Jackson) for important Treasury offices. The newspaper, in salty small town editorial fashion, said that if the cabinet member "requires a 'yes man' we may expect Mr. Jackson back in Jamestown at an early date." Independence was always a basic element of his character, as witness his opposition to our armed involvement in World War I, and in many a political position taken by this outspoken Democrat in a strongly Republican community. One of his proud boasts about his beloved city of Jamestown was that it was "a city where everyone is free to speak in support of any ism that one likes." He put this to many tests, including his

successful defense of strikers accused of rioting. It is interesting in our own day to recall that he was instrumental
during World War I in preventing in Jamestown any of the
so-called slacker raids then in vogue with an extremist few.

Another Jackson characteristic was humility. Frank G.
Raichle, now a famous advocate, provides this anecdote. In
Jackson's Buffalo period (several months in 1917–18) he
was one of the trial lawyers for the local tram lines, which
sported the grandiose corporate name of International
Railway Co. Raichle, an even-younger lawyer, succeeding
Jackson in this uneasy occupation, asked Jackson why he
was leaving Buffalo. With all sincerity the answer was that
Buffalo was too large a city. Jackson, who was to reach the
topmost heights, thought that he could find success only in
a smaller town. Another illustration of his innate humility
appeared when Secretary Morgenthau offered him his first
Washington assignment as General Counsel of the Internal Revenue Bureau, and Jackson was with some difficulty
persuaded that he was of sufficient ability for it. He had
some humor, too. In a case he handled in the Supreme
Court about 1936 for the Treasury, he was trying to collect
a tax deficiency on the ground that a gift of money by an
aged citizen was taxable as a gift in anticipation of death.
Justice McReynolds, renowned for caustic questioning,
asked Mr. Jackson if it were not true that the taxpayer at
the time of the transfer was a vigorous Scotsman with
many years of life in sight. The young Treasury counsel replied: "Exactly so, your Honor. And on this point the Government bases its case. Being a Scotsman, the respondent
would not have given away his money except in anticipation of death." Even McReynolds laughed. During the
presidential campaign of 1932 I had my own little experi-

ence of this saving grace of humor. I had the post—or at least the title—of Erie County Campaign Manager for FDR. One day in the office of the local Democratic leader I was told by him that Mr. Roosevelt and State Chairman James A. Farley were sending to Buffalo for observation of our local campaign procedures a Mr. Jackson, a name quite unknown to me. Peevishly I complained at this intrusion by some unknown outsider, and suggested that this inspector was unnecessary and unwelcome. While I was thus unburdening myself I was introduced to a bystander who turned out to be Jackson. He had a good laugh about it and afterward became my good friend.

A life that was full of greatness began when Robert H. Jackson came into the world as the son of William Eldred Jackson and Angeline Houghwout Jackson on February 13, 1892, in Spring Creek, Warren County, Pennsylvania, near the New York State border and on the same farm where his father and grandfather had been born. Until he left for Washington in 1934, he lived for practically his whole youth and early manhood in Chautauqua County, New York, in a scenic hill and lake country which he loved and whose people he loved, along what in earlier days had been the pathway of American history from Lake Erie toward the Mississippi. His ancestors on his father's side were Connecticut-born pioneers, the first white settlers of Spring Creek, and all Democrats. His mother's parents were descendants of early Dutch settlers in this state. On his father's side there was a great-grandfather whose father was a British barrister and an officer of the Middle Temple, of which Robert H. Jackson became an honorary bencher. Robert's father was a small businessman whose activities included horse-breeding and horse-trading, and the son's

familiarity with and love for horses and horsemanship en-
dured into his days in Washington, to which he trans-
ported his favorite riding horses. He never lost his boyhood
love for outdoor sports. Once he and his daughter Mary
went on a two-week pack horse trip through the wild Saw-
tooth Mountains in Montana. He enjoyed hiking, ice skat-
ing, and in his Jamestown days, boating on lovely Chautauqua Lake. Some of his happiest days were with his wife,
son, and daughter in a colonial-type house on the lake just
outside Jamestown, where he owned a small farm where he
kept his horses, cruised the lake in his cabin cruiser, regularly attended the meetings of the Saturday Night Club in
Jamestown, and exercised at local public meetings his natural talents as a public speaker.

Young Robert's early schooling was in Spring Creek and
in Frewsburg, New York, where he moved when five years
old, and in Jamestown, New York. While attending Jamestown High School (as a post-graduate student in 1909
–1910 after graduation from Frewsburg High School) he
sat in the classes of an unusual teacher, Mary Willard, who
trained and encouraged her young student in the reading of
the classics and in debating and English composition, help-
ing him to develop a notable capacity for writing and
speaking clear, simple, direct English. He often spoke of his
gratitude to Miss Willard and other teachers at Jamestown
and Frewsburg who helped to make him a omnivorous
reader for all his life. It was appropriate that after his death
a committee arranged for setting up at Frewsburg High
School a Jackson Memorial Fund to encourage students to
excellence in history and the art of debate. Late in life,
reminiscing about his high school experiences, Jackson
spoke of the days "when the girls wore more clothes and

less make-up, when the country boys and girls carried their lunches, and when dances and parties broke up at about the time they now begin."

Before I turn to Robert Jackson's lawyer days in Jamestown, let me refer briefly to a vignette furnished me by a man who for two years was his schoolmate and shared with him a double desk in the old frame schoolhouse in Frewsburg. In 1901 Frewsburg was a quiet village with wooden sidewalks, and streets that were dusty in summer and muddy most of the rest of the year. There was a Liberty Pole and a town pump, iron railings in front of the local emporia, and sheds in the rear wherein to tie or stable the horses of the farmers who came to town to trade. The churches too had sheds for the horses, buggies, and teams of their communicants, and these "church sheds" were great places for little boys like Bob Jackson to play hide-and-seek and other games. The only exciting times were when horses ran away or when the wonted calm was broken by a revival meeting in one of the churches. The nearest city was Jamestown, but travel there required a train ride plus a trolley trip. Robert Jackson's father ran the Frewsburg livery stable as well as the hotel where Robert lived at the time he shared the classroom desk with my chronicler. One of the Jackson boy's pleasures and privileges was to ride his father's horses around the village. Many Civil War veterans lived in quiet Frewsburg then and many the war tales they told to wide-eyed boys. When Robert was still in school there, a new electric railroad from Jamestown reached Frewsburg, and its construction brought surveyors, laborers, engineers, noise and excitement, and shiny new cars.

At one end of the village was a canning factory which in season employed people of all ages preparing peas, corn, beans, and pumpkins for the market. When Robert Jackson and his friend were about twelve years old they sought jobs at the cannery and got them, at eleven cents per hour each, sometimes for fourteen hours on Saturdays. Robert had at least one other job, mowing lawns at five cents per lawn. That same year the two boys enrolled as pupils with a traveling singing school master whose course involved ten evenings of instruction plus a grand concert at the end. Neither boy achieved operatic status and both were stationed in a rear row at the grand concert. I suppose there is much in this account that is nostalgic and perhaps apochryphal, but it does evoke a picture of the kind of quiet village life that produced a country lawyer who became a national leader of political thought and action, Cabinet member and Supreme Court Justice, and the chief prosecutor representing the United States of America at Nuremberg in the greatest criminal trial the world has known.

But always in Jackson there was a lot of Frewsburg, and it is right and good that his burial was in the Jackson family plot in a quiet rural cemetery in that hamlet. After a life of accomplishment and service he returned in death to the quiet hills of home.

Our country lawyer's law life began in 1913 when, at the age of 21, he was admitted to the bar after a year at Albany Law School (attending, too, some sessions of the New York Court of Appeals) plus study in the Jamestown office of his cousin, Frank Mott. (In a lecture at Stanford University Jackson once spoke of himself as "a vestigial remnant of the system which permitted one to come to the bar by way of apprenticeship in a law office.") Then, married to the lovely Irene Alice Gerhardt, whom he had met in Albany, young Bob, unaided by fame, friends, or family connections, hopefully opened his own little law office in Jamestown (assisted by an eight-dollar-a-week stenographer), in which city he continued to practice (except for the brief Buffalo interval) until he left for Washington and national office in 1934. Meanwhile he had fathered two children, Mary (now Mrs. Craighill) and William Eldred Jackson, whose attainments as a lawyer and citizen are well known. After a few years of solo practice he entered successive partnerships, the last of which was Jackson, Herrick, Durkin, and Leet.

Jackson was the complete small-city lawyer, jury lawyer, equity lawyer, appellate lawyer in over fifty appeals, one who could act as counsel for and director of banks, utilities, and other businesses, as well as labor unions, while finding time to win locally famous cases (one in malpractice, the other against the city for causing a typhoid epidemic). He also won a locally significant false imprisonment cause, and fought successfully a criminal anarchy charge against a communist for peddling the *Daily Worker* in Salamanca, N. Y. All the while he remained an outspoken Democrat in a strongly Republican community, getting to know Franklin D. Roosevelt, refusing offers to join Buffalo and New York law firms, spending much time in bar association affairs and civic problems. He read omnivorously, was active in his Episcopalian parish and in Masonry, was sometime Corporation Counsel appointed by a Republican mayor of Jamestown. Living through the Great Depression, he was thereby inspired to examine more closely the history and laws of economics.

This is one chapter in the life history of Bob Jackson, small town lawyer who traveled long and far from the hill country of southwestern New York to the marbled halls of

Washington; from a village boyhood to the inner councils of the National Government and a seat on the world's most powerful judicial tribunal; from small city law practice to arguing before the Supreme Court some of the most significant constitutional issues ever litigated in America; from justice of the peace courts in Chautauqua County to the War Trials Tribunal at Nuremburg; from the representation of little people in little courts to representing the world's conscience at an international judgment seat. And along that long road and to its end he traveled as a country lawyer. In his way he embodied a significant part of the American dream—the storybook American boy who by brains and work and pluck drives himself from an unpromising start to a glorious finish. But I think Jackson himself would have been wryly amused at such a picture. I think he would rather be remembered as a lawyer of his time and place who by obeying his code lived a useful, happy life and died an honored citizen.

Every life leaves lessons for those who follow—and Robert Jackson's life was too full of lessons for full telling here. Let me try to give you a part of his lesson for those who survive him in the profession he practised so well and loved so much. First of all, he proved that the copybook maxims still have validity, and that hard work, endless study, clear thinking, courage, loyalty to clients, associates, and career, sacrificial community and public services, plus a good humor and absence of pretense—old-fashioned and unsophisticated virtues though they be—are still the marks of the useful lawyer, in high place or low, in Frewsburg or Jamestown, Wall Street or State Street, Washington or London.

Jackson was all his life a New York State lawyer, loyal to

his guild and concerned for its well-being. What is the most useful of the lessons he left to lawyers as a group? I think it lay in his life-long consciousness of the group needs of his craft, in his long, tireless advocacy of stronger, more inclusive, more truly representative organization of New York State lawyers and in his awareness of the need for simplification and modernization of the New York State Court system, the largest such system on earth. When Bob Jackson was thirty-five years old he was one of the organizers of, and became the second president of, the Federation of Bar Associations of Western New York (the first president was Jackson's close friend Philip J. Wickser of Buffalo, who gave so much of his time to unselfish efforts for the better organization of the bar). Jackson never lost his interest in that Federation or in the New York State Bar Association, or in the Jamestown Bar Association of which he was once president. He was before his time in urging an all-inclusive organization of all the lawyers in the state—a so-called integrated bar such as exists in California, Florida, Wisconsin, and some twenty-three other states, large and small.

Robert H. Jackson was prophetic and far-thinking too in his insistence more than thirty years ago on an idea that even today is not accepted by some lawyers—that the New York State court complex must somehow be made into a truly unified system. Speaking in 1932 to the Judicial Section of the New York State Bar Association while he was serving as a member of a Commission set up by Governor Roosevelt to study the courts, Jackson complained that "the whole vast system moves with no central authority, without even conference between one court and the other, and the machine tends simply to fly apart." "A far-sighted program" he said, "would seem to call for abolishing several courts, of unifying them, centralized control and administrative supervision and erecting, instead of a museum of odd courts of all sizes and degrees of usefulness, a simple, compact judicial system." Thirty years ago our prophet cried out in a trackless wilderness of apathy. In the last dozen years we have seen a little daylight. Our memorialization of Robert Jackson should include an examination of our collective conscience to see whether we are giving full support to today's efforts to develop in this state a truly modern court system.

Final illustration of Jackson's remarkable prescience and vision as to the future of law is that in New Deal days he foresaw and prophesied, to the usual chorus of scoffing, that the time would come, as it is now coming with the War on Poverty programs, when government would pay for legal advice and legal service to the poor. On this occasion, however, the prophet was without honor, at least to a newspaper columnist whose sour comment was: "Mr. Jackson had better come back to Jamestown and private law. He might get back to earth again—on the other side of the fence."

It is frustrating and futile to try to describe such a man in a single phrase, but Eugene Davidson did pretty well in his recently published monumental treatise on the Nuremberg Trials, in which he called Robert H. Jackson "a man of urgent idealism." I see him as a practical dreamer, holding fast to one of the best and oldest dreams of our race— the dream of prompt and equal justice for all the members of our free society. It was fitting that when he was sworn in as Justice of the United States Supreme Court in 1941 his hand rested on a century-old family Bible opened at a paragraph in Deuteronomy which reads thus:

"And I charged your hearts at that time, saying, hear the causes between your brethren and judge righteously between every man and his brother and the stranger that is with ye. Ye shall not respect persons in judgment but ye shall hear the small as well as the great; ye shall not be afraid of the face of man; for the judgment is God's; and the cause that is too hard for you bring it unto me and I shall hear it.

I conclude with an incident typical of the man. Long ago on a summer evening I attended at Jamestown a dinner given by Chautauqua County people in honor of their townsman, Supreme Court Justice Robert H. Jackson. As has been known to occur at such exercises, one of the diners had exceeded his beverage quota and was expressing his affection for the guest of honor by ill-timed interruptions of the speeches. An officious committee member intervened by attempting to escort the out-of-order member out of doors. Justice Jackson would have none of that. He not only announced from the dais that the heckler must be allowed to remain, but also in a quiet, friendly tone informed the bibulous one that he must be quiet so that he and the guest of honor could enjoy the rest of the evening together. Kindliness and charm prevailed, and all was thereafter serene. Thus was the country lawyer, Robert Houghwout Jackson, at home with the people who loved and trusted him.

CHARLES S. DESMOND

Mr. Justice Jackson
and Individual Rights

PROFESSOR PAUL A. FREUND

With an Introduction by

THE HONORABLE CHARLES D. BREITEL

About a month ago we had the privilege of hearing the first of the lectures by Chief Judge Charles S. Desmond. I should say former Chief Judge Charles S. Desmond of the Court of Appeals of New York, who was introduced by John Lord O'Brian.

I want to say immediately that John Lord O'Brian's introduction on that occasion was so magnificent, by a man already 92 years of age, that no introducer ever to follow him could possibly attempt its like.

That first lecture was devoted to the early professional life of Robert Jackson in Jamestown and in Buffalo.

Tonight's speaker, Professor Paul Freund, will discuss another aspect of Judge Jackson's career. It will deal with the protection of individual rights as conceived and as developed in that very special philosophy that was that of Robert Jackson.

Now, I thought that it would be interesting to you if you would know how this series came about.

The one who first suggested the series was the late Mr. Justice Felix Frankfurter.

It is particularly interesting that it was Felix Frankfurter who first made the suggestion, and this has something to do with the choice of the speaker for tonight, because of the two men in the Supreme Court of the United States at that time, there weren't any two who were more kindred spirits than Robert Jackson and Felix Frankfurter.

There was really something special about the relationship between them, and the very fact that it was Judge Frankfurter who suggested the series tells you that.

It is also true that you would recognize immediately that Judge Frankfurter—and I say this with all of the maximum admiration that I have for Judge Frankfurter—was not one lightly to have this kind of respect and affection for another man, unless that man was quite worthy of it. The interesting thing is that Paul Freund, our speaker for tonight, is a very special link between these two men. Paul Freund of course was also at Harvard when Felix Frankfurter was making that school famous.

Paul Freund, after he left Harvard, went into government. It was there and last in the Solicitor General's office that he was associated with Robert Jackson. They became personal and professional and ideological intimates.

Too much time has not passed, and those involved personally in the life and the works of Mr. Justice Jackson may yet recall him. This is true of Judge Desmond, who was associated with him in the early years; it is very true of John Lord O'Brian; it is true of Paul Freund and of the Right Honorable Lord Shawcross, who was Attorney General of Great Britain and was also chief British counsel at the Nuremberg Trials, at the same time that Mr. Jackson was chief United States prosecutor.

One of the things that I've been able to learn about the relationship between Judge Frankfurter and Judge Jackson, is that the two of them often reached the same views and the same conclusions and the same results in cases, but by entirely different ways.

Felix Frankfurter, with that highly sophisticated, analytic, conceptualistic approach that was his, rooted in reality, to be sure, but nevertheless, highly abstract, would twit Judge Jackson for reaching his results by a much more empirical, humanist approach. And he used to say of Judge Jackson that he was utilizing Jamestown jurisprudence.

Paul Freund, after he left Harvard, went into government in several agencies, and it was in those agencies and later in the Solicitor General's office that he was associated with Robert Jackson. They became personal and professional and ideological intimates. Paul Freund is particularly qualified, almost uniquely qualified, to develop the broader philosophic aspects of Judge Jackson's thinking and achievements in the Supreme Court.

I talked with several close associates of Professor Freund, and when I tried to pin them down to specifics, they said this was not possible because he was a man whose catholicity of interests was so great that to say of him that he was a specialist, or that he had a specialty, was to completely distort the perspective that one might have of him.

When I tried to verify this further—although I really shouldn't have needed a verification; I was being the careful lawyer—I learned that he was president of the American Academy of Arts and Sciences, an organization concerned with the whole range, the whole spectrum, of the sciences physical, and social, and of philosophy. There is no area in the universe of knowledge or understanding that he does not claim as his own.

When Paul Freund was first made university professor at Harvard University, he insisted upon teaching in the college. He is not satisfied to confine his interests or his concerns to the professional field in which he is such a master. That world was just too small for him. We get a key to that in a lecture that he gave some years ago at Washington University, in which he developed a paradox. It is usually said that the social sciences have so much to contribute to law in its discipline. Freund said no, it was much more important that our law and our discipline contribute what it had to contribute to general education in the universities.

Typical of him, he insisted that the lawyers, because of their own expertness, had the burden of carrying this teaching, this infiltration, if you like, into general education, and this explains why he has insisted upon teaching in the college and bringing to general education the law and its discipline which he reveres so much.

Paul Freund was born in 1908. That I can tell you from personal experience is a vintage year. Not only was I born in that year and my wife as well, but the President of the United States and the Governor of New York. So 1908 is a very good year. I commend it to you. Although those of you who have been born later are much better off. He received his bachelor's degree from Washington University and his law degree from Harvard. He then clerked for Judge Brandeis and thereafter until 1939 was in the Treasury Department and later in the Solicitor General's Office. Since 1939 he has been teaching continuously and lecturing at Harvard University and throughout the country.

He is the one man, or at least one of the two or three men, who have contributed more to our understanding of both the Supreme Court and the constitutional process, and I have deliberately distinguished the two, although they sometimes get confused, to give us an understanding of exactly what is involved.

He has also treated particularly of the great justices of the Supreme Court in his own time. Currently, he is the editor-in-chief of a history of the Supreme Court which involves a great number of informed experts in the field.

As an observer and student of the Supreme Court, he has been both an admirer and a bold critic. There was a great similarity in his and Mr. Justice Jackson's philosophies and approaches. Paul Freund, like Robert Jackson, was no absolutist and I would like to read to you something that Paul Freund wrote in the Pennsylvania Law Review some twenty years ago. I think it gives a marvelous text about the law, about jurisprudence, and of course about the man who would say these things. Here are his words:

In a larger sense, all law resembles art for the mission of each is to impose a measure of order on the disorder of experience without stifling the underlying diversity, spontaneity and disarray. New vistas open in the art as in law. In neither discipline will the craftsman succeed, unless he sees that proportion and balance are essential; that order and disorder are both virtues when held in a proper tension. The new vistas give a false light unless there are cross lights. There are, I am afraid, no absolutes in law or art except intelligence.

As an additional confidence that Paul Freund is especially qualified to discuss the philosophy of Judge Jackson with respect to individual rights, when the Supreme Court, after the untimely decease of Judge Jackson, held memorial services, Paul Freund was one of the speakers. When the Stanford Law Review published an issue in memory of Judge Jackson, easily the most distinguished piece in that issue was that by Paul Freund.

We have an interesting situation here. You do not have

to rely on what I think about Paul Freund. We know what Judge Jackson thought about him. In the preface to his book entitled The Struggle for Judicial Supremacy, Judge Jackson wrote that he was heavily indebted to Paul Freund for many helpful criticisms of his text. Freund headed the staff of the Solicitor General's Office from 1933 to 1939, and the government briefs during this critical period bore the impress of his scholarship and judgment. Judge Jackson, he said, turned to his counsel from habit.

CHARLES D. BREITEL

Having served under Robert Jackson while he was Solicitor General, I can pay him the ultimate accolade bestowed by one lawyer upon another. As a junior who worked on a number of briefs from which he made the oral argument in the Supreme Court, without fail I was enthralled and engrossed to sit at counsel table and listen admiringly to the argument. This is an experience that, as lawyers will agree, rarely comes to a junior who is put in that vis-a-vis position with his senior.

Justice Brandeis used to say that Solicitor General Jackson ought to be made Solicitor General for life. Fortunately, the President did not hear that advice.

When Jackson became a Justice, it was, in turn, a delight to argue before him. He had a capacity for breaking tension in the courtroom. When, for example, a lawyer who had been arguing intensely for a considerable period said, "May I be advised how much time remains? The clock at the front and the one at the rear of the courtroom seem not to agree," Justice Jackson quipped, "That's the influence of this Court."

I remember arguing a case before him on behalf of the War Department. In those days, our Executive Departments did not have euphemistic names. It was a very odd case. The Quartermaster Corps, anxious to acquire very quickly a large plot of land in Missouri for an artillery range, employed an agent there to buy up parcels of land on a commission, which was fixed at 5 percent of the purchase price agreed on. The more he agreed to pay, the greater his remuneration! There was, to be sure, some formal approval required for these contracts in the War Department. When the Department of Justice heard about the arrangement, they promptly ordered the contracts cancelled and instituted eminent domain proceedings; but some of the landowners objected, standing on their contracts.[1]

From the outset of my argument for the Government in the Court, Justice Jackson was not very sympathetic. He said, "Week after week the Government comes before us and tells us that we must respect administrative discretion —and now you are telling us that we should overturn administrative discretion." And I responded, rather feebly, "But I submit there is a difference between discretion and indiscretion." That didn't seem to move him. Then, bringing up my best card, I referred to something in the record. There had been a meeting of the landowners in Kansas City to discuss their position, and a debate developed. When one of the men said that this contract had been approved by the Department of Justice, another replied, "That's impossible. Attorney General Jackson"—who at the time had been head of the Department—"Attorney General Jackson is too smart a lawyer for that." Well, Jus-

[1] Muschany v. United States, 324 U.S. 49 (1945).

tice Jackson smiled faintly at the compliment and said, "Even that doesn't persuade me." He ultimately disqualified himself.

As a judge, Robert Jackson displayed what I would call, summarily, a dialectical mind—recognizing principles in collision. His thinking was not one-dimensional, all warp and no woof. He bore no resemblance to the boy who said he knew how to spell "banana" but didn't know when to stop. Judge Jackson would thoroughly have agreed with the celebrated passage of Justice Holmes: [2]

All rights tend to declare themselves absolute to their logical extreme; yet all in fact are limited by the neighborhood of principles of policy which are other than those on which the particular right is founded, and which become strong enough to hold their own when a certain point is reached.

By temperament, I suspect, this kind of thinking, this kind of inner tension, was congenial to him. For although, as those who knew him were well aware, he was the most congenial and gregarious and companionable of men, he still retained an inner reserve of privacy, a kind of temple of the spirit, into which strangers and friends were not bidden to enter. The private and the public sectors, I think he would have said, called for recognition as fully in the human personality as they do in political economy.

Against this general background, I should like to discuss two topics: Justice Jackson's treatment of problems under the First Amendment, and his treatment of issues of procedural guarantees in the Bill of Rights.

When I speak of the First Amendment, I speak, of course, loosely, to include similar guarantees against the states. He had very interesting things to say about this,

[2] Hudson Water Co. v. McCarter, 209 U.S. 349, 355 (1908).

about the possible differences between the scope of Bill of Rights guarantees as against the national and the state governments, particularly because of the different responsibilities which each government held with regard to the maintenance of peace and order. But this is a topic which Justice Stewart will deal with later in this series, and so I will talk about First Amendment guarantees without stopping to deal with the element of federalism.

Justice Jackson's great theme in interpreting the First Amendment was the inviolability of the nonconformist mind and the private conscience. But even here the dialectical analysis remains. The theme was struck when these interests of privacy and conscience were used as a shield. The countertheme was struck when they were used as a sword which might threaten the social fabric. In tracing this counterpoint through specific cases I need hardly offer an apology, because Justice Jackson was, above all—and this was one of his great strengths—a case lawyer.

I start, naturally, with the flag salute case, in which Justice Jackson found himself in very sharp disagreement with his good friend, Justice Frankfurter.[3] It was a case enmeshed in the war against fascism, and from both sides— from the side of the government in the concern for national unity; on the side of the defendants in their conjuring up the image of a Nazi salute. Superficially, one would think of the case as presenting a problem of religious freedom, of the free exercise of religion: an eccentric notion, if you will, on the part of the Jehovah's Witnesses of what was God's and what was Caesar's—eccentric from the standpoint of general community definition.

But Justice Jackson lifted the case, or, at any rate, trans-

[3] West Virginia State Bd. of Educ. v. Barnette, 319 U.S. 624 (1943).

formed it, from an issue of religious freedom into the issue
of the basic authority of government to compel a person to
profess a belief that he does not hold. In this special sense,
Justice Jackson insisted that there was a constitutional right
of silence. He said this:[4]

To sustain the compulsory flag salute, we are required to say
that a Bill of Rights which guards the individual's right to speak
his own mind left it open to public authorities to compel him
to utter what is not in his mind.

It is just a step from the flag salute case to a requirement
that one hold a certain belief in order to hold a union
office. In the case of the Taft-Hartley loyalty oath, Justice
Jackson drew a bright line between an oath of nonmember-
ship in the Communist Party, which he thought was legitimate as a condition of union officership, and an oath of
nonbelief in the purposes of the party. In the *Douds* case
he described the line in this way: [5]

I think that under our system, it is time enough for the law to
lay hold of the citizen when he acts illegally, or, in some rare
circumstances, when his thoughts are given illegal utterance.
I think we must let his mind alone.

This, of course, was not an altogether easy position to
maintain. An oath is required on the part of an appointee
to the Tennessee Valley Authority Board that he believe in
the purposes of the Tennessee Valley Authority. And I
assume that an oath could be required of Secret Service
men that they entertain loyal beliefs regarding their government. But Justice Jackson saw a more generalized threat
to the noncomformist's thought which was not warranted

[4] *Id.* at 634
[5] American Communications Assn. v. Douds, 339 U.S. 382, 444 (1950).

by any danger to the social order that could not be met through sanctions directed against conduct. He added: [6]

Progress generally begins in skepticism about accepted truths. The danger that citizens will think wrongly is serious, but less dangerous than atrophy from not thinking at all. Thought control is a copyright of totalitarianism, and we have no claim to it. It is not the function of our government to keep the citizen from falling into error; it is the function of the citizen to keep the government from falling into error.

When belief is more than a shield, when it is not quite a sword but perhaps a trumpet call, what was Justice Jackson's response?

That issue was raised by the case involving a requirement that a paid union organizer secure a card of identity from the state capital if he was planning to solicit membership in any union organization. Justice Jackson concurred in the decision upsetting a conviction for speaking without applying for or acquiring such a permit or card, and he said this: [7]

It is not often in this country that we now meet with direct and candid efforts to stop speaking or publication as such. Modern inroads on these rights come from associating the speaking with some other factor which the state may regulate so as to bring the whole within official control. Here, speech admittedly otherwise beyond the reach of the states is attempted to be brought within its licensing system by associating it with solicitation. Speech of employers otherwise beyond reach of the Federal Government is brought within the Labor Board's power to suppress by associating it with coercion or domination. Speech of political malcontents is sought to be reached by associating it with some variety of sedition. Whether, in a particu-

---

[6] *Id.* at 422–43.   [7] Thomas v. Collins, 323 U.S. 516, 547 (1945).

lar case, the association or characterization is a proven and valid one, often is difficult to resolve. If this Court may not—or does not—in proper cases inquire whether speech or publication is properly condemned by association, its claim to guardianship of free speech and a press is but a hollow one.

And so he joined the majority in differentiating the kind of solicitation which was a general appeal for the cause of unionism from a more limited solicitation which involved the seeking of funds or a commitment to pay.

But even where funds are solicited, the question arises whether the government may go beyond identification and inquire into beliefs to determine their truth or the sincerity with which they are held. This was the problem raised by the so-called "I Am" case from California, where the federal mail fraud statute was used to convict the leaders of this eccentric religious sect.[8] A majority of the Court held that the prosecution was legitimate, provided the jury was not asked to pass on the truth or falsity of the religious claims of the defendants, but only on their sincerity.

Justice Jackson, dissenting, took the view that this was an altogether impractical distinction from the standpoint of a jury—that a jury called upon to determine sincerity or insincerity of the leaders of an eccentric religious sect would inevitably be influenced by its own conception of what was true or false, credible or incredible, in the domain of religious experience. Furthermore, Justice Jackson said, "So far as the victims are concerned, what is really involved here is not so much the mulcting of them in a financial way, but rather if there is a wrong, it is imposing on their religious credulity"—and with this he thought the Court should have nothing to do. "I would dismiss the indict-

---

[8] United States v. Ballard, 322 U.S. 78 (1944).

ment," he said, "and have done with this business of judicially examining other people's faith" [9] —a statement reminiscent of the one quoted from the Douds case. "We must let his mind alone," even though the beliefs were considerably more active and aggressive than in the cases first discussed.

After these four cases, the flag salute, the Taft-Hartley oath, the card of identity, and religious fraud, we should move on to cross Justice Jackson's line to the employment of beliefs as a sword.

We may start with a modest controversy over the doorbell-ringing ordinance applied against Jehovah's Witnesses. The majority held that this ordinance which made it an offense to ring door bells, uninvited, in order to solicit even for religious causes, was an undue suppression of the individual's right to receive a message, as well as of the proselytizer's right to deliver it.[10] Justice Jackson referred to this case in his Godkin lectures at Harvard and summarized it in this way, explaining his dissenting position: [11] "If the Court holds that the right of free speech includes the right to enter upon private property and summon the owner to the door, it necessarily holds that a majority of a community are without the right to protect their hours of rest against such religiously inspired aggression."

Actually, it has seemed to me that the controversy was of a lesser magnitude than that, and really involved the problem whether the municipality must rely on the ordinary law of trespass, including criminal trespass, depending on

[9] *Id.* at 95.

[10] Murdock v. Pennsylvania, 319 U.S. 105 (1943); Martin v. Struthers, 319 U.S. 141 (1943).

[11] R. H. Jackson, The Supreme Court in the American System of Government, Harvard University, Godkin Lectures (1955).

an individual occupant's notice, or whether the municipality may insulate everyone, willing or unwilling, from the approaches of Jehovah's Witnesses. If you look at it in this light, the dilemma posed by Justice Jackson is not as striking as he makes it out to be, for the city is not helpless; it could enforce a trespass law, though to be sure it would be more difficult to administer.

May a state apply child labor laws to a family of Jehovah's Witnesses selling their literature as they deem it their religious duty to do? Justice Jackson, as might have been expected, approved the application of the child labor laws to the activities of the Witnesses on the streets in selling their literature; and yet he dissented from the decision affirming their conviction.[12] His reason was this—that having decided very recently in the door-bell-ringing case that proselytizing, seeking converts and seeking funds outside of the membership, was an essential element of religious practice, the Court could not rationally distinguish this case from the other. He lamented the door-bell-ringing result. He would welcome the different result reached in this case but he thought the Court could not honestly reach it without overruling the door-bell-ringing decision, and since they were unwilling to do that, he dissented. He said: "I think the limits of individual immunity begin to operate whenever the activities begin to affect or collide with the liberties of the public. Religious liberties or activities which concern only members of the faith are and ought to be free—as nearly and absolutely free as anything can be." [13]

His dissent here evidences a not uncharacteristic trait, a kind of "throw it back on the others" or "rub it in" posi-

[12] Prince v. Massachusetts 321 U.S. 158 (1944).   [13] *Id.* at 176.

tion which was a kind of puritanical response to what struck him as intellectual disingenuousness.[14]

To move along the spectrum of aggressive activities, one encounters the Jehovah's Witnesses case on the use of sound trucks—what would constitutional law do if Jehovah's Witnesses suddenly disbanded—where the chief of police was vested with authority to grant a license without any explicit standards to govern his action. In a prosecution for using a sound truck without a license, a majority of the Court held that the use of the sound truck could not be so punished.[15] Justice Jackson dissented, arguing that if, as he believed, a city could prohibit sound trucks entirely, it could do the lesser thing of permitting them upon the approval of an administrative officer. He tended to overlook or minimize the problem of inherent arbitrariness in the statute and the maxim that was a favorite of my mentor, Thomas Reed Powell, that by doing less than it might the state sometimes does more than it may. It is the more surprising on Justice Jackson's part because elsewhere he was extremely sensitive to claims of arbitrary or discriminatory action as a denial of equal protection of the laws. The explanation may be that he was unwilling to assume such admin-

[14] Compare his treatment of the issue of government employees as jurymen in criminal cases in the District of Columbia. He regarded them as disqualified for bias, but was in a minority. Frazier v. United States, 355 U.S. 497, 514 (1948). When, later, the Court was asked to hold such jurors improper in a prosecution for contempt of the House Un-American Activities Committee, he refused to accept that position so long as the Court adhered to the general holding of the Frazier case: "I agree that this highlights the unfairness of the Frazier rule and provides a reason for overruling it; but I do not agree that it justifies the proposed exemption to that decision." Dennis v. United States, 339 U.S. 162, 174 (1950). "Whenever any majority can be mustered to overrule that weird and misguided decision, I shall be one of it." *Id.* at 173.

[15] Saia v. New York, 334 U.S. 558 (1948).

istration of the statute without a record to support that danger. What perhaps prevailed in the end in this case was his lawyer's instinct for the case—that the mere existence of the statutory discretion was not enough to excuse the Witnesses unless they could show that it had in fact been abusively administered.

Justice Jackson's position, as I have said, is somewhat surprising in the light of his sensitivity to equal protection claims. Some twenty years ago, in another case from New York, not involving the First Amendment, he expressed very candidly and interestingly his view of the two clauses —due process and equal protection. Justice Holmes used to say that the equal protection clause is the last refuge of a constitutional lawyer. Today it is more likely to be the first instinctive reaction of a constitutional lawyer. Justice Jackson twenty years ago—before the burgeoning of equal protection, before the school desegregation case in fact— said: [16]

My philosophy as to the relative readiness with which we should resort to these two clauses, due process and equal protection, is almost diametrically opposed to the philosophy which prevails on this Court. The burden should rest heavily upon one who would persuade us to use the due process clause to strike down a substantive law or ordinance. Invalidation of a statute or ordinance on due process grounds leaves ungoverned and ungovernable conduct which many people find objectionable. Invocation of the equal protection clause on the other hand does not disable any governmental body from dealing with the subject at hand. The framers of the Constitution knew and we should not forget today that there is no more effective practical guarantee against arbitrary and unreasonable government than to require that the principles of law which officials

[16] Railway Express Agency v. New York, 336 U.S. 106, 111 (1949).

would impose upon a minority must be imposed generally. Conversely, nothing opens the door to arbitrary action so effectively as to allow those officials to pick and choose only a few to whom they will apply legislation and thus to establish the political retribution that might be visited upon them if larger numbers were affected.

A similar problem arose with regard to the use of public parks under a municipal permit or licensing system. In the Kunz case, from New York, a renegade minister had engaged in provocative, insulting, personally abusive outdoor speech which resulted in physical disorder, and when he applied for a renewal of his permit to use the streets and parks it was denied. The statute, however, contained no standards either for the granting, revocation, or renewal of such a permit. The Court, as it had done in the sound truck case, reversed a conviction for speaking without a license, and again Justice Jackson dissented, more concerned with the actual case than with potential abuses under the statute.[17] He took occasion wryly to chide the Court for its insistence on adequate standards in the drafting of such ordinances or statutes. "Of course," he said,

standards for administrative action are always desirable and the more exact the better, but I do not see how this Court can condemn municipal ordinances for not setting forth comprehensive First Amendment standards. This Court never has announced what those standards must be; it does not now say what they are; and it is not clear that any majority could agree on them.[18]

In the same case, on the use of the public park, he wielded the stiletto again, pointing out that recently in the case from New York on released time for religious instruc-

[17] Kunz v. New York, 340 N.Y. 290 (1951).   [18] *Id.* at 308.

tion in the public schools, the Court had held that public property *may not* be made available to a religious group for religious instruction,[19] while in the Kunz case they were holding that public property *must* be made available to a religious speaker for purposes of his cause. Occasionally Justice Jackson paid a certain price for his wit which only a pedant or professor would stop to cavil at; but, being both, I have to say that perhaps the fairer schoolhouse analogy would have been to the use of school property after class hours by a religious group where the property was also available to nonreligious groups.

We have approached the more degrading forms of religion through the Kunz case and we probably reach the nadir in the Terminiello case from Illinois, the case of the suspended priest who aroused an audience in a hall with a harangue that fully sustained the tone of the opening words: "Now, I am going to whisper my greetings to you, Fellow Christians. . . . I said 'Fellow Christians,' and I suppose there are some of the scum got in by mistake, so I want to tell you a story about the scum. . . . And nothing I could say tonight could begin to express the contempt I have for the slimy scum that got in by mistake." This to a crowd consisting partly of sympathizers and partly of hostile listeners, with the foreseeable result of physical disorder and violence within and without. The trial judge charged the jury that Terminiello was liable for inciting a breach of the peace if his conduct was such as to stir the public to anger, invite dispute, bring about a condition of unrest, or create a disturbance. A majority of the Supreme Court seized on this charge, though it had not been objected to in

[19] Illinois ex rel. McCollum v. Board of Education, 333 U.S. 203 (1948).

the state courts, as interfering with freedom of expression, because the very purpose of protected speech under the First Amendment, it was said, is to create unrest and disturbance of the mind.[20]

This was too much for Justice Jackson, who again focused on the actual case and had no doubt that in its context no one, including the jury, could have been misled by the use of the words in the charge. He said: [21]

This Court has gone far toward accepting the doctrine that civil liberty means the removal of all restraints from these crowds, and that all local attempts to maintain order are impairments of the liberty of the citizen. The choice is not between order and liberty; it is between liberty with order and anarchy without either. There is danger that if the Court does not temper its doctrinaire logic with a little practical wisdom it will convert the constitutional Bill of Rights into a suicide pact.

The opinion, I think it is clear, reflects his preoccupation with European totalitarianism through his experience at Nuremberg, where he had been made profoundly aware of what happened when crowds whipped up into hatred fought for control of the streets. Perhaps in view of that experience it should not be too surprising that he concurred in affirming the conviction of Dennis in the leading case under the Smith Act.[22] At the same time it should be pointed out that he could not accept the reasoning of the majority, which attempted to fit the case into the clear and present danger criterion by recasting the test as a kind of sliding scale, the gravity of the danger discounted by its improbability. Justice Jackson must have felt that this was standing the test on its head. What he did was circumvent

20 Terminiello v. Chicago, 337 U.S. 1 (1949).   21 *Id.* at 37.
22 Dennis v. United States, 341 U.S. 494 (1951).

the clear and present danger test by emphasizing the element of conspiracy in the case. This is rather surprising in view of some other attitudes of his, which I will mention in a moment, about the law of conspiracy. It is fair to observe, however, that he had his misgivings about the Smith Act and prosecutions under it. He said: [23] "While I think there was power in Congress to enact this statute and that as applied in this case it cannot be held unconstitutional, I add that I have little faith in the long range effectiveness of this conviction to stop the rise in the Communist movement."

Another kind of measure associated with the European fascist experience is the group libel law. In a criminal conviction coming up from Illinois, the Beauharnais case, the leading opinions were by Justice Frankfurter for the Court sustaining the conviction, and by Justice Black for the dissenters urging reversal.[24] Those two opinions take polar positions. For Justice Frankfurter the Illinois group libel law was essentially no different than a private libel law. For Justice Black the pamphlets which the defendant circulated, referring to Negroes as users of marijuana and rapists and wielders of knives, and distributed in an effort to keep Negroes out of white property districts, were exemplars of freedom of expression in its classic form and not essentially different from the Spectator papers of the eighteenth century. It is greatly to Justice Jackson's credit as a lawyer and judge that he was dissatisfied with both positions and tried to grapple with the case more concretely. I cannot think of a better example of his distinctive lawyerlike approach to a case—craftsmanship infused with a sense of history and philosophy as well.

In this case Justice Jackson recognized the special re-

[23] *Id.* at 577–78.
[24] Beauharnais v. Illinois, 343 U.S. 250 (1952).

sponsibility of local governments for the maintenance of public order, even against aggressions that are verbal: [25]

Group libel statutes represent a commendable desire to reduce sinister abuses of our freedoms of expression—abuses which I have had occasion to learn can tear apart a society, brutalize its dominant elements, and persecute even to extermination its minorities. While laws or prosecutions might not alleviate racial or sectarian hatreds and may even invest scoundrels with a specious martyrdom, I should be loath to foreclose the states from a considerable latitude of experimentation in this field. Such efforts, if properly applied, do not justify frenetic forebodings of crushed liberty, but these acts present most difficult policy and technical problems as writers who have canvassed the problem more comprehensively than is appropriate in a judicial opinion have well pointed out.

Then he proceeds to an examination of appropriate safeguards in the special case of group libel, which partakes in part of ordinary libel but also in part of political expression. He finds the Illinois statute wanting in a great many of these basic safeguards. It included no criterion of specific intent to create disorder, or of clear and present danger of producing disorder. There was no provision for the defense of truth, or, if the matter was not factual, even for the defense of fair comment. And finally, it was left to the judge to determine, presumably in his instructions to the jury, whether the matter was or was not libelous—a throwback or at least an echo of the old common law of seditious libel against which American lawyers fought in the eighteenth century. On balance, he concluded that the Illinois statute was too deficient in its procedures to warrant the conviction under it.

The group-libel case can serve as a bridge between the

[25] *Id.* at 304.

area of the First Amendment and the other principal field I
wish to cover—constitutional guarantees of fair procedure
in the enforcement of the criminal law. Here again the
figure of the shield and the sword may be a useful clue to
Justice Jackson's thinking. Guarantees designed to protect
the accused from an unfair trial—one in which the search
for truth is deflected by governmental abuses—must be
stoutly enforced as defenses against conviction; other guarantees, designed for their collateral effect on police conduct, might not serve as defenses but only as a weapon to
be employed against the official malefactors.

The line between the two was sharply drawn in the Irvine case from California, involving a particularly repug-
nant form of eavesdropping. Evidence was obtained
through the installation of a microphone in a bedroom.
The Court upheld the resulting conviction as not violate of
federal law.[26] Justice Jackson took the position that the admission of the evidence did not affect the integrity of the
search for truth; but he was so outraged by what had been
done that he took the extraordinary step of suggesting in
his opinion that the Court refer the record to the Attorney
General of the United States for appropriate action under
the Civil Rights Acts.[27]

Similarly, when faced with the problem of exclusion of
Negroes from a grand jury, he took the view that there was
no actual harm if a petit jury which later convicted had
been properly constituted, and that the remedy for improper selection of the grand jury must be sought elsewhere, presumably through some form of civil or criminal
action under the Civil Rights Acts—the sword and not the
shield.[28]

[26] Irvine v. California, 347 U.S. 128 (1954).   [27] Id. at 137–38.
[28] Cassell v. Texas, 339 U.S. 282 (1950).

When there was an actual affront to procedural decency in the trial itself or in administrative proceedings, Justice Jackson was at his most eloquent and vehement. In a spirit reminiscent of Justice Brandeis in cases, for example, of entrapment, Justice Jackson insisted that due process was required not merely for the sake of the defendant but also for the sake of the integrity of the administration of justice. It was a symbol, I think he would have said, that government is worthy of the monopoly of force that it exerts, that we protect ourselves no less than the defendant by insisting on due process of law and that only thus are judges able to endure the agony and absurdity of human decision. He said:

Procedural fairness, if not all that originally was meant by due process of law, is at least what is most uncompromisingly required. Procedural due process is more elemental and less flexible than substantive due process. It yields less to the times, varies less to the conditions, and defers much less to legislative judgment. Let it not be overlooked that due process of law is not for the sole benefit of the accused. It is the best insurance for the government itself against those blunders which leave lasting scars on a system of justice but which are bound to occur on ex parte considerations. Compare *Knauff v. Shaughnessy*, which was a near miss, saved by further administrative and congressional hearings from perpetrating an injustice.[29]

The *Knauff* case was the well-known war bride case, raising an issue of secrecy, in which Justice Jackson took the buttons off the foil: [30]

Now this American citizen is told he cannot bring his wife to the United States but he will not be told why. He must abandon his bride to live in his own country or forsake his country to live with his bride. So he went to court and sought a writ of

[29] Shaughnessy v. United States ex rel. Mezei, 345 U.S. 206 (1953).
[30] Knauff v. Shaughnessy, 338 U.S. 537 (1953).

habeas corpus, which we never tire citing to Europe as the unanswerable evidence that our free country permits no arbitrary official detention, and the government tells the court that not even a court can find out why the girl is excluded. It says that we must find that Congress authorized this treatment of war brides and even if we cannot get any reasons for it we must say it is legal. Security requires it. Security is like liberty in that many are the crimes committed in its name. The menace to the security of this country, be it as great as it may, from this girl's admission is as nothing compared to the menace to free institutions inherent in procedures of this pattern. In the name of security the police state justifies its arbitrary oppressions on evidence that is secret because security might be prejudiced if it were brought to light in hearings. The plea that evidence of guilt must be secret is as abhorrent to free men because it provides a cloak for the malevolent, the misinformed, the meddlesome, and the corrupt to play the role of informer —undetected and uncorrected.

And when a similar issue of secrecy was raised in another immigration case he said: [31]

[31] Shaughnessy v. United States ex rel. Mezei, 345 U.S. 206, 219 (1953).
It was in another deportation case that Justice Jackson made his celebrated recantation of a position he had taken as Attorney General:
Precedent, however, is not lacking for ways by which a judge may recede from a prior opinion that has proven untenable and perhaps misled others. See Chief Justice Taney, License Cases, 5 How. 504, recanting views he had pressed upon the Court as Attorney General of Maryland in Brown v. Maryland, 12 Wheat. 419. Baron Bramwell extricated himself from a somewhat similar embarrassment by saying, "The matter does not appear to me now as it appears to have appeared to me then." Andrews v. Styrap, 26 L.T.R. (N.S.) 704, 706. And Mr. Justice Story, accounting for his contradictions of his own former opinion, quite properly put the matter: "My own error, however, can furnish no ground for its being adopted by this Court. . . ." United States v. Gooding, 12 Wheat. 460, 478. Perhaps Dr. Johnson really went to the heart of the matter when he explained a blunder in his dictionary—"Ignorance, sir, ignorance." But an escape less self-depreciating was taken by Lord Westbury, who, it is said, rebuffed

This man who seems to have led a life of unrelieved insignificance must have been astonished to find himself suddenly putting the Government of the United States in such fear that it was afraid to tell him why it was afraid of him. Government counsel argued that Ellis Island is his refuge whence he is free to take leave in any direction except west. This might mean freedom if only he were an amphibian.

We pass from secrecy to its opposite—publicity. In a case which anticipates several recent *causes célèbres*, *Shepherd v. Florida*, he wrote separately, the rest of the Court reversing *per curiam* on the ground that Negroes had been excluded from the jury.[32] Justice Jackson regarded that element in the case as relatively trivial compared with the rest of the record. It showed a particularly horrible crime committed by Negroes against a white girl. Newspaper stories reported confessions obtained from the accused, although no confession was ever sought to be introduced.

Every detail of these passion-arousing events was reported by the press under such headlines as "Night Riders Burn Lake Negro Homes," and "Flames From Negro Homes Light Night Sky In Lake County." These and many other articles were highly prejudicial, including a cartoon published at the time of the grand jury picturing four electric chairs and headed "No Compromise—Supreme Penalty." Counsel for the defendants made two motions, one to defer the trial until passions had died out, and the other for a change of venue. These were denied. The Supreme Court of Florida, affirming the conviction, ob-

a barrister's reliance upon an earlier opinion of his Lordship: "I can only say that I am amazed that a man of my intelligence should have been guilty of giving such an opinion." If there are other ways of gracefully and good-naturedly surrendering former views to a better considered position, I invoke them all.

McGrath v. Kristensen, 340 U.S. 162, 177-78 (1950).

[32] Shepherd v. Florida, 341 U.S. 50 (1951).

served that "The inflamed public sentiment was against the
crime with which the appellants were charged rather than
defendants' race." Such an estimate seems more charitable than
realistic. The situation presented by this record is not different
in essentials from that which was found a denial of due process
in *Moore v. Dempsey*.[33]

And he concludes on a deeply felt note: "To me, the
technical question of discrimination in the jury selection
has only theoretical importance. The case presents one of
the best examples of one of the worst menaces to American
justice. It is on that ground that I would reverse." [34]

Finally, I would mention two more general contributions
of Justice Jackson to the criminal law, one having to do
with the law of conspiracy and the other of *mens rea*. I
refer to two cases in which he wrote some of his most
scholarly and potentially influential opinions.

The conspiracy case reflected once again his Nuremberg
experience. He was greatly impressed by the fact that his
civil law colleagues were unfamiliar with the notion of conspiracy and with the fact that it derived from the English
Star Chamber, and now he pointed out that whatever its
proper realm might be, it was being expanded in a way that
produced very loosely tried cases and potential miscarriages
of justice. The case was that of a panderer charged with
two co-conspirators, both women, of conspiracy to trans-
port one of them from New York to Florida for immoral
purposes. He raises the question why this was not simply
tried under the Mann Act. The conspiracy charge enabled
the prosecutor to introduce, or he thought it did, an incriminating hearsay declaration by one of the women co-
conspirators against the defendant Krulowitz made six

---

[33] *Id.* at 53–54.   [34] *Id.* at 55.

months after the travel in question. It was presented and admitted on the theory of an implied conspiracy to conceal the crime, the notion of constructive continuing conspiracy. Justice Jackson tore this notion apart, characterizing the proceeding as a dragnet operation. "Few instruments of injustice," he said, "can equal that of implied or presumed or constructive crimes." [35]

The other contribution, having to do with *mens rea*, came in the Morissette case, raising a problem of statutory construction under a statute which punished the taking of Government-owned property without explicitly requiring a specific intent to steal.[36] The defendant maintained that he understood the property to have been abandoned by the Government, and the question was whether he could be convicted nonetheless on the theory that no *mens rea* was required by the terms of the statute. Justice Jackson took occasion to philosophize about the nature and objectives of the criminial law and produced what is quite possibly the best opinion we have on that subject. There are few opinions, to be sure, which do essay some inquiry into the peculiar aims of the criminal law, an inquiry that has considerable bearing on current debates over whether punishment is obsolete. Justice Jackson, reading into the law a requirement of blameworthiness, recognized that this element related not merely to an objective of primitive retribution, but also to a wholesome and humane limitation on the governmental power of coercion and constraint, furnishing a warrant that the stigma of the criminal law was being legitimately applied.

What, in sum, was the legacy of Justice Jackson in the

[35] Krulewitch v. United States, 336 U.S. 440, 457–58 (1949).
[36] Morissette v. United States, 342 .S. 246 (1952).

realm of individual rights? I have tried to suggest that his was a brand of realism and philosophic reflection which had been nourished by experience in affairs and by wide, thoughtful reading, particularly in history and political philosophy. He was enmeshed in the case at hand and yet did not find the case confining. Indeed, I think he found it strengthening and liberating because through the case he was able to focus and intensify the light of philosophy.

This philosophic realism was encased in burnished words, was conveyed with a kind of Elizabethan gusto for the swordplay of wit. The combination is irresistible to students of law. No modern judge more surely delights and engrosses students, whether or not they are in agreement, then does Justice Jackson.

The Justice contrived to focus on the twin evils that are most corrupting in a legal order: secrecy where there should be disclosure; publicity where there should be privacy. It is, I suggest, remarkable that he perceived by intuition these two besetting sins and summoned up against them his most fervent and poignant attack.

More generally, he left a legacy of concern for the inner self, the free mind and spirit on which a free society ultimately depends. In an era of growing exploration and manipulation of the deepest recesses of the mind, as well as the far reaches of outer space, a time of increasing anonymity and submersion in the mass, a period of a morality of statistics, a poignant reminder from Justice Jackson of who each of us is—the vagrant, mysterious, unservile, yet responsible self—is a heritage to be husbanded and treasured.

PAUL A. FREUND

Robert H. Jackson's Influence on Federal-State Relationships

THE HONORABLE POTTER STEWART

With an Introduction by

THE HONORABLE JOHN M. HARLAN

Federal-state relations figured prominently in the constitutional thinking of Mr. Justice Jackson, and no worthier exponent of his views in this field could have been chosen than Mr. Justice Stewart. The subject is also a very timely one at a moment when constitutional changes are taking place at a rapid pace.

The basic tenet of our political system is that a free society is best assured by a diffusion of governmental power. Constitutionally, that principle has two aspects: a separation of power within the federal system among the Legislative, Executive, and Judicial branches; and, second, reservation to the States, or to the people, of all powers not delegated to the Federal Government nor prohibited to the States. The first of these stemmed primarily from considerations of political philosophy; the second was born out of the necessities of achieving union. In their subsequent development, both of these aspects of the Constitution have combined to serve, in different ways, as barriers to the creation of a central overriding political authority in this country.

No field of constitutional law has given rise to more important litigation or led to greater differences of opinion among judges and lawyers than what has been referred to in some Supreme Court opinions as the "delicate balance" between federal and state authority. The preservation of that balance becomes the more difficult at times when great social or economic changes are taking place in the country, for in such times those who do not see the federal system as a strong pillar of political liberty tend to become impatient with the slowness of its workings, and with the existence of different patterns among the States with respect to things about which they feel strongly. Federal authority is then looked to as the best means for bringing about prompt and pervasive change. In this respect the period of Mr. Justice Jackson's government service is not unlike the present era.

The time which found Mr. Justice Jackson in Washington saw a wide extension of federal authority based principally upon an expanded interpretation of the Commerce Clause. Following in the wake of the great depression of 1929 and the early 1930s, broad new fields of federal economic regulation, respecting matters theretofore considered to lie within state control, were begun under the aegis of this broadened view of the Commerce power. At the same time, however, the Court exhibited a sensitive concern for state authority in other directions. The Court continued to back away from the notion of "substantive" due process, a constitutional doctrine under which important state legislative enactments had from time to time been invalidated under the Due Process Clause of the Fourteenth

Amendment. Federal judicial oversight of state legislation has now become a very rare thing under the Due Process Clause. And while the concepts of "procedural" due process remained intact, the Court was for the most part prone to exercise authority in such matters quite sparingly. This was also true with respect to the Equal Protection Clause of the Fourteenth Amendment. In short, while the Jackson period witnessed a substantial extension of federal authority into what had previously been regarded as purely state domains, the source of that extension is to be found principally in an expanded view of the powers affirmatively delegated by the Constitution to the Federal Government, rather than in an expansion of the restrictions placed by the Fourteenth Amendment upon state action.

The period following Mr. Justice Jackson's death has seen still further constitutional inroads upon state authority, this time primarily as a result of judicial applications of the Fourteenth Amendment. This development has had three aspects: first, a greatly enlarged view of the reach of the Equal Protection Clause of the Fourteenth Amendment; second, a growing acceptance of the previously rejected view that the Fourteenth Amendment "incorporates" most, if not all, of the provisions of the Federal Bill of Rights, making them applicable as such against the States; and, third, interpretations of some of those provisions to encompass governmental action heretofore not thought to be within their purview. Overriding all of these constitutional attributions is a nebulous, yet discernible, view that the Constitution through judicial interpretation should be made to serve as an instrument for achieving basic reforms where other avenues for change are for one reason or another foreclosed.

In combination these developments have resulted in bringing within the sweep of federal power much that has hitherto been left to the States. The most wide-ranging impacts have been in the fields of criminal law and of state legislative apportionment, and I do not think that it can be said that the end is yet in sight. From the standpoint of the subject under consideration this evening the important thing, I think, is not so much whether the particular changes themselves are good or bad as it is the fundamental shift such changes evince in the current judicial approach to federal-state relationships. This shift must be recognized as involving something more than mere differences among judges as to where the line should be drawn between state and federal authority in particular cases arising under the Fourteenth Amendment. It reflects, I believe, at bottom a distrust in the capabilities of the federal system to meet the needs of American society in these fast-moving times, and a readiness on the part of the federal judiciary to spearhead reform without circumspect regard for constitutional limitations upon the manner of its accomplishment. To those who see our free society as dependent primarily upon a broadening of the constitutional protections afforded to the individual, these developments are no doubt considered to be healthy. To those who regard the federal system itself as one of the mainsprings of our political liberties, this increasing erosion of state authority cannot but be viewed with apprehension. There can be little doubt, I venture to say, that were Mr. Justice Jackson still here, he would be found among the latter.

Mr. Justice Potter Stewart was born in Jackson, Michigan, on January 23, 1915. He attended the Hotchkiss

School, and thereafter was graduated cum laude from Yale University in 1937 and from the Yale Law School in 1941, a year of study at Cambridge University, England, having intervened between college and law school. He practiced law in New York City from 1941 to 1942, and again from 1945 to 1947 following his return from more than three years of service in the Navy during World War II. Thereafter he practiced law in Cincinnati, Ohio, from 1947 to 1954. In the latter year President Eisenhower appointed him to the United States Court of Appeals for the Sixth Circuit, on which he served until 1958, when he was appointed, again by President Eisenhower, an Associate Justice of the Supreme Court of the United States. As one whose own judicial career has manifested a sensitive concern for striking an appropriate balance between federal and state authority in the varied contexts in which that question has arisen, Mr. Justice Stewart is admirably fitted to write on that aspect of Mr. Justice Jackson's constitutional philosophy.

JOHN M. HARLAN

Thirteen years ago this month, at the very outset of the Court's 1954 Term, an untimely death [1] took Mr. Justice

[1] "Justice Jackson had suffered a previous attack in the spring of 1954 and had spent several weeks in a hospital in Washington and recuperating at his beautiful home, Hickory Hill, at McLean, Virginia. His doctors gave him the choice between years of comparative inactivity or a continuation of his normal activity at the risk of death at any time. With characteristic fortitude he chose the second alternative. He returned to his work on the Court, sat at the session of May 17, 1954, and joined in the unanimous opinion of that date in the school segregation cases. After a restful summer vacation at his home, at the Bohemian Grove in California and on a fishing

Robert H. Jackson [2] from the Supreme Court of the United
States. He had taken his seat there just thirteen years earlier, on the first Monday of October in 1941.[3]

I never knew Robert Jackson in his lifetime. Chief Judge
Desmond, Professor Freund, and Lord Shawcross all had
the happy experience of sharing with him a close personal
association during some period of his life. I did not. In
1941, the year he came to the Court, I was graduated from
law school. When he died in 1954, I was a very new member of a federal court in the midwest.

But from the day I came to Washington four years later,
I have felt his presence in a very personal way. The Supreme Court, despite the necessarily close association of its
members, can be an extraordinarily impersonal place. The
names of those who have gone, even recently gone, are seldom spoken. But not so the name of Robert Jackson. Many
times I have heard a colleague open his conference discussion of a case by recalling what "Bob Jackson used to say
about this kind of a problem." Many times I have heard
Albert the elevator man smilingly speak of "Mr. Justice
Jackson" with a happy mixture of affection and respect.

---

trip in Canada, he returned for the present term of the Court and sat at
its opening session on Monday, October 4." Proceedings in the Supreme
Court of the United States in Memory of Mr. Justice Jackson, 349 U.S.
XXVII, at XXIX.

[2] There was another Mr. Justice Jackson. Howell E. Jackson of Tennessee,
appointed by President Benjamin Harrison, served as an Associate Justice
from March 4, 1893, until his death on August 8, 1895. On at least one
occasion Mr. Justice Robert Jackson noted with approval the views of his
earlier namesake. See Jackson, The Struggle for Judicial Supremacy (1941),
p. 47.

[3] Attorney General Jackson had become Mr. Justice Jackson during the
Court's summer recess in 1941. He was nominated as an Associate Justice
by President Roosevelt on June 12, 1941, and his nomination was confirmed by the Senate on July 7. Four days later he was commissioned and
took the oath of office.

And, far from Washington, in a great California Redwood forest called the Bohemian Grove, where, as in other summers, Robert Jackson went in the last summer of his life, many times I have heard him remembered with stories of his humor and his humanity.

Yet I personally know him only as some day all must know him—through the legacy of his written words.[4] In my years as a young circuit judge I very soon came to know him as an engaging teacher. In my time as a member of the Supreme Court I have known him as a congenial and persuasive colleague.

The late Mr. Justice Burton used to like to say that the nine members of the Supreme Court work there each day not only with one another, but with all the Justices who have gone before—with the Justices "in the books."[5] Whatever poetic license there may be in that general statement,[6] I can think of no better way to describe the particular relationship I feel with Mr. Justice Jackson.

His direct and pungent style has been described by other speakers in this series of lectures. Because he was able to express what he had to say with such singular clarity and force, he never left any doubt about where he stood on any issue, and why. And because of that extraordinary gift, there shines through the pages of his writing not just his intellect, but the whole power of his personality.

I direct my remarks to the subject of Mr. Justice Jackson and the relationships between the States and the Federal

[4] Of the 14 Justices with whom Mr. Justice Jackson served, only three remain members of the Court.

[5] See, e.g., 33 A. B. A. Journal 645 (1947).

[6] When Mr. Justice Thurgood Marshall took his seat in October, 1967, he became the 96th Justice in the history of the Supreme Court. The present Justices thus have 87 predecessors, and I confess to difficulty in remembering even the names of some of them.

Government, or perhaps more precisely, his understanding of the essential balance of those relationships under the Constitution of the United States. It seems to me his views upon that large subject reflect his whole vision of our constitutional structure, and of the Supreme Court's function in preserving that structure's integrity.

It is important, I think, to begin with an understanding of Justice Jackson's deeply held views about the basic role of the Supreme Court in American life. To do this we need not, as we must with most Justices, piece together passages from judicial opinions or attempt to draw inferences from judicial decisions. For Justice Jackson fully expressed his beliefs in two published volumes. Perhaps uniquely, the first of these was published on the very eve of his appointment to the Court, and the second at the very end of his years of service there.

The first book was called *The Struggle for Judicial Supremacy*. In it Robert Jackson chronicled the epic confrontation in the mid-1930s between a New Deal President and a Supreme Court relentlessly opposed to much of that President's legislative program.[7]

The second book consisted of three lectures that Robert Jackson wrote in the last months of his life, to be delivered as the Godkin Lectures at Harvard during the following academic year. The lectures were never given, but they were published after the author's death in a volume called

[7] By the time the book was published in 1941, President Roosevelt's proposal to "reorganize the federal judiciary," as he put it, had, of course, already passed into history. The episode continues to be a subject of lively interest. See, e.g., Baker, Back to Back (1967); Leuchtenburg, The Origins of Franklin D. Roosevelt's "Court-Packing" Plan, 1966 Supreme Court Review 347 (Kurland ed.).

The Supreme Court in the American System of Government.

The earlier book was the story, told in restrained anger, of a Court that

took over into its control the whole range of the national economy . . . tried to . . . make the teachings of *lassez faire* a part of our constitutional law . . . [and] conjured up such doctrines as "freedom of contract" to defeat legislation, though the Court later found that the Constitution did not mention it.[8]

It was the story of a Court that "in just three years, beginning with the October 1933 term . . . refused to recognize the power of Congress in twelve cases." [9] And it was the story of a Court that, in the era before 1937, had used the Due Process Clause of the Fourteenth Amendment to strike down economic and social legislation of the individual States no less than 228 times.[10]

Last summer I reread *The Struggle for Judicial Supremacy.* Although the book tells of events that took place hardly thirty years ago, it seems today to speak of "old, unhappy, far-off things, and battles long ago." In short, it is, superficially, a curiously dated book. Just how dated may be gathered from one brief passage: "[N]ever in its entire history can the Supreme Court be said to have for a single hour been representative of anything except the relatively

[8] The Struggle for Judicial Supremacy, pp. 37–38.   [9] *Id.* at 41.

[10] "Beginning about 1890, it was a fortunate and relatively innocuous piece of reform legislation that was able to run the gantlet of the due process clause. Two hundred and twenty-eight times thereafter the Supreme Court set aside state legislative action under the Fourteenth Amendment. The figures do not tell the whole story, because a single decision may have caused the death of similar legislation in many states and prevented its birth in others." *Id.* at 50.

conservative forces of its day." [11] Yet, beneath the surface
there runs a theme of timeless significance in the political
structure of our national life. The importance of the book
for purposes of the moment lies in its disclosure of the
foundation for the author's convictions about the necessary
limits of judicial power.

In the last two chapters Robert Jackson spoke clearly of
the inherent limitations he saw upon what even the wisest
Supreme Court could achieve, and of the tragic damage
that could be inflicted by trying to achieve too much—
damage to the Court itself, to the law, and to the Nation.

In the final chapter his convictions about the Court's
proper mission were expressed in these words:

The Supreme Court can maintain itself and succeed in its
tasks only if the counsels of self-restraint urged most earnestly
by members of the Court itself are humbly and faithfully
heeded. After the forces of conservatism and liberalism, of
radicalism and reaction, of emotion and of self-interest are all
caught up in the legislative process and averaged and come to
rest in some compromise measure . . . , a decision striking it
down closes an area of compromise in which conflicts have
actually, if only temporarily, been composed. Each such decision takes away from our democratic federalism another of
its defenses against domestic disorder and violence. The vice
of judicial supremacy, as exerted for ninety years in the field
of policy, has been its progressive closing of the avenues to
peaceful and democratic conciliation of our social and economic
conflicts.

In stressing this I do not join those who seek to deflate the
whole judicial process. It is precisely because I value the role
that the judiciary performs in the peaceful ordering of our

11 *Id.* at 187.

society that I deprecate the ill-starred adventures of the judiciary that have recurringly jeopardized its essential usefulness.

Nor am I unmindful of the hard-won heritage of an independent judiciary which for over two hundred years has maintained the "rule of law" in England, the living principle that not even the king is above the law. But again, the rule of law is in unsafe hands when courts cease to function as courts and become organs for control of policy. . . .[12]

These were the views of Robert Jackson as he came to the Supreme Court in 1941. What were his views thirteen years later, in the light of his own experience as a member of the Court, and of his singular experience at Nuremberg, where he had looked tyranny full in the face? As he himself once observed, the years can "play havoc with one's philosophy." [13] They did not play havoc with his. This is what he wrote in the closing months of his life, in what was to be the last of the Godkin Lectures:

The political function which the Supreme Court, more or less effectively, may be called upon to perform comes to this: In a society in which rapid changes tend to upset all equilibrium, the Court, without exceeding its own limited powers, must strive to maintain the great system of balances upon which our free government is based. Whether these balances and checks are essential to liberty elsewhere in the world is beside the point; they are indispensable to the society we know. Chief of these balances are: first, between the Executive and Congress; second, between the central government and the states; third, between state and state; fourth, between authority, be it state or national, and the liberty of the citizen, or between the rule of the majority and the rights of the individual.

12 *Id.* at 321–22.
13 *Id.* at 44. The reference was to Charles Evans Hughes.

I have said that in these matters the Court must respect the limitations on its own powers because judicial usurpation is to me no more justifiable and no more promising of permanent good to the country than any other kind. So I presuppose a Court that will not depart from the judicial process, will not go beyond resolving cases and controversies brought to it in conventional form, and will not consciously encroach upon the functions of its coordinate branches. . . .[14]

Upon this understanding of Robert Jackson's consistent vision of the institutional function of the United States Supreme Court, we may turn to his view of the proper constitutional balance in the relationship between "the central government and the states," remembering always his clear awareness that a most powerful instrument of that "central government" could be the Supreme Court itself.

As to one aspect of that relationship, Justice Jackson came as close to being doctrinaire and absolute as it was possible for him to be. No man ever came to the Court with a larger concept of the federal commerce power than did this man who had so recently watched in dismay as a Court with a niggardly view of that power had repeatedly struck down vital national legislation. In the great federalist tradition of John Marshall, he clearly believed that only if the commerce power is given full sweep can we truly call ourselves citizens of a nation.

His first concurring opinion as a Justice was written in a case striking down a California law that made it a criminal offense to bring any person into that State who was without means of support.[15] Justice Jackson relied in that case on

<hr />

[14] The Supreme Court in the American System of Government, at 61–62.

[15] Edwards v. California, 314 U.S. 160, 181. Cf. Steinbeck, *The Grapes of Wrath.*

the Privileges and Immunities Clause, rather than the Commerce Clause, but his opinion made clear his concept of nationhood. Some of you will remember its closing lines:

Rich or penniless, Duncan's citizenship under the Constitution pledges his strength to the defense of California as a part of the United States, and his right to migrate to any part of the land he must defend is something she must respect under the same instrument. Unless this Court is willing to say that citizenship of the United States means at least this much to the citizen, then our heritage of constitutional privileges and immunities is only a promise to the ear to be broken to the hope, a teasing illusion like a munificent bequest in a pauper's will.[16]

His sweeping concept of congressional power under the Commerce Clause was never more manifest than in the opinion he wrote for the Court in the case of *Wickard v. Filburn* in the 1942 Term.[17] The decision in that case, upholding the power of Congress to tell a small Ohio farmer how much wheat he could grow, even for his own use, remains a high water mark of congressional commerce power even today,[18] and as such continues to invite enthusiastic critical attack.[19] What is more to the point of the present discussion, however, is the other side of the coin—the uncompromising duty Justice Jackson felt to overturn any state law that encroached upon the economic nationalism he believed the Commerce Clause fully protected and guaranteed. In a rather unimportant case that came to the Court from Arkansas during his first Term, he filed a separate opinion serving clear notice of what his attitude toward such state laws was consistently going to be:

16 *Id.* at 185–86.   17 317 U.S. 111.
18 Cf. Heart of Atlanta Motel, Inc. v. United States, 379 U.S. 241.
19 See Whittaker, Charles E., "A Confusion of Tongues," 51 A. B. A. Journal 27, 32 (1965).

Our national free intercourse is never in danger of being suddenly stifled by dramatic and sweeping acts of restraint. That would produce its own antidote. Our danger, as the forefathers well knew, is from the aggregate strangling effect of a multiplicity of individually petty and diverse and local regulations. Each may serve some local purpose worthy enough by itself. . . . But to let each locality conjure up its own dangers and be the judge of the remedial restraints to be clamped onto interstate trade inevitably retards our national economy and disintegrates our national society. It is the movement and exchange of goods that sustain living standards, both of him who produces and of him who consumes. This vital national interest in free commerce among the states must not be jeopardized.

I do not suppose the skies will fall if the Court does allow Arkansas to rig up this handy device for policing liquor on the ground that it is not forbidden by the commerce clause, but in doing so it adds another to the already too numerous and burdensome state restraints of national commerce and pursues a trend with which I would have no part.[20]

Perhaps the most extreme reach of Justice Jackson's views came in the 1948 Term when he wrote the Court's opinion holding that New York could not constitutionally restrict the export of milk to Massachusetts.[21] His opinion reviewed at length the history of the Commerce Clause and of its interpretation by the Court, and repeated a now familiar theme:

Our system, fostered by the Commerce Clause, is that every farmer and every craftsman shall be encouraged to produce by the certainty that he will have free access to every market in the Nation, that no home embargoes will withhold his exports, and no foreign state will by customs duties or regulations exclude

20 Duckworth v. Arkansas, 314 U.S. 390, 401–402.
21 Hood & Sons v. Du Mond, 336 U.S. 525, 539.

them. Likewise, every consumer may look to the free competition from every producing area in the Nation to protect him from exploitation by any. Such was the vision of the Founders; such has been the doctrine of this Court which has given it reality.[22]

Four Justices dissented in that case, and one of the dissenting opinions accused the majority of arbitrarily striking down the New York law in a manner reminiscent of the old Court's actions under the Due Process Clause.[23] But for

[22] Justice Jackson's vision of the Commerce Clause remained unobscured throughout his judicial service. See, e.g., Northwest Airlines v. Minnesota, 322 U.S. 292, 302 (concurring opinion); Independent Warehouses v. Scheele, 331 U.S. 70, 91 (dissenting opinion).

The theme was struck a final time in the last of the Godkin lectures: "I think it is a mistake to lump all states' rights together as is done so frequently in political discussions.

"There can be no doubt that in the original Constitution the states surrendered to the Federal Government the power to regulate interstate commerce, or commerce among the states. They did so in the light of a disastrous experience in which commerce and prosperity were reduced to the vanishing point by states discriminating against each other through devices of regulation, taxation and exclusion. It is more important today than it was then that we remain one commercial and economic unit and not a collection of parasitic states preying upon each other's commerce. I make no concealment of and offer no apology for my philosophy that the federal interstate commerce power should be strongly supported and that the impingement of the states upon that commerce which moves among them should be restricted to narrow limits." The Supreme Court in the American System of Government, at 66–67.

[23] "The judicially directed march of the due process philosophy as an emancipator of business from regulation appeared arrested a few years ago. That appearance was illusory. That philosophy continues its march. The due process clause and commerce clause have been used like Siamese twins in a never-ending stream of challenges to government regulation. . . . The reach of one twin may appear to be longer than that of the other, but either can easily be turned to remedy this apparent handicap. . . . Both clauses easily lend themselves to inordinate expansions of this Court's power at the expense of legislative power. For under the prevailing due process rule, appeals can be made to the 'fundamental principles of liberty and justice' which our 'fathers' wished to preserve. In commerce clause cases reference can appropriately be made to the far-seeing wisdom of the 'fathers' in guard-

Justice Jackson, striking down a state law under the Commerce Clause was "a wholly different thing." [24] Quite simply, he perceived in the Commerce Clause a guarantee of economic nationalism so clear as to confer upon the Court an essentially creative role in preserving that economic nationalism even at the cost of the invalidation of encroaching local laws. [25] But he could find in the Due Process Clause of the Fourteenth Amendment no comparably definable mandate.

By the time Justice Jackson came to the Court in 1941, the particular struggle over the Due Process Clause that he had recorded in *The Struggle for Judicial Supremacy* had come to an end. The battle had been won. No longer would the Court find in the Fourteenth Amendment authority to strike down state laws enacted in the broad inter-

---

ing against commercial and even shooting wars among the states. Such arguments have strong emotional appeals and when skillfully utilized they sometimes obscure the vision." 336 U.S., at 562–63 (dissenting opinion of Mr. Justice Black).

[24] See Duckworth v. Arkansas, 314 U.S. 390, 401.

[25] Justice Jackson's strong "federalist" position was not limited to the Commerce Clause. In his Cardozo Lecture before this Association, he outlined a construction of the Full Faith and Credit Clause that would have allowed for the creation of a "truly national system of justice" paralleling the national economic system grounded in the Commerce Clause. Jackson, Full Faith and Credit—The Lawyer's Clause of the Constitution, 45 Col. L. Rev. 1 (1945). While fully endorsing the Court's recognition in Erie R. Co. v. Tompkins, 304 U.S. 64, of the States' primacy in formulating substantive rules of common law, he would not have followed *Erie* when the question involved a choice of law between two interested jurisdictions with conflicting rules. In short, he disagreed with the rule of Klaxon v. Stentor Mfg. Co., 313 U.S. 487. See Wells v. Simonds Abrasive Co., 345 U.S. 514, 519 (dissenting opinion). In these situations the constitutional objective, he thought, should be the perfection of a " 'more perfect union' of our legal systems," not the preservation of uniformity of decision within the forum state. 45 Col. L. Rev., at 27.

est of social welfare.[26] Gone was the discredited doctrine of "freedom of contract." Gone too was the notion that the Due Process Clause was little more than a free translation of the Justices' own views with respect to the wisdom or need of a particular state law.

But was the basic constitutional struggle really over, or had it simply shifted to a new arena? In that deeply troubling question there lay for Justice Jackson a formidable challenge of principle. His response to that challenge was, it seems to me, courageous and clear. It is in the context of cases arising in the area of the criminal law that his response to the challenge can perhaps most sharply be traced, but I would suggest that those cases no more than illuminate his whole constitutional understanding.

In order to appreciate the full force of Justice Jackson's due process beliefs, it is important, I think, to begin by recalling the punctilious standard he always applied in the review of criminal cases coming from the federal courts. In cases invoking the Supreme Court's general supervisory power over the administration of justice in the federal judicial system, Justice Jackson gave free rein to his own scrupulous and imaginative concern for the highest concepts of fair play. Many of you will remember his dissent in a case from the District of Columbia where the defendant had been convicted by a jury composed entirely of government employees. The opening lines of that dissenting opinion are

[26] That authority has not been resurrected, see Ferguson v. Skrupa, 372 U.S. 726, nor has its passing generally been lamented. See McCloskey, Economic Due Process and the Supreme Court: An Exhumation and Reburial, 1962 Supreme Court Review 34 (Kurland ed.); cf. Struve, The Less-Restrictive-Alternative Principle and Economic Due Process, 80 Harv. L. Rev. 1463 (1967).

animated with the incisive bite that so often sharpened his style. He said:

On one proposition I should expect trial lawyers to be nearly unanimous: that a jury, every member of which is in the hire of one of the litigants, lacks something of being an impartial jury. . . . This criminal trial was an adversary proceeding, with the Government both an actual and nominal litigant. It was the patron and benefactor of the whole jury, plus one juror's wife for good measure.[27]

This is not the occasion for an exhaustive review of Supreme Court decisions, but at least two other cases invoking the Court's supervisory power are worth mentioning. One was a case involving a man called Krulewitch, an obscure panderer who had been convicted of conspiracy to violate the Mann Act.[28] Justice Jackson seized the occasion to write a concurring opinion in which he inveighed, eloquently and with great force, against the abuse of conspiracy prosecutions in the federal courts.[29] It was a scholarly opinion, but it reflected as well his characteristically practical insight. He said this:

A co-defendant in a conspiracy trial occupies an uneasy seat. There generally will be evidence of wrongdoing by somebody. It is difficult for the individual to make his own case stand on its own merits in the minds of jurors who are ready to believe that birds of a feather are flocked together. If he is silent, he is taken to admit it and if, as often happens, co-defendants can be prodded into accusing or contradicting each other, they convict each other. . . .[30]

---

[27] Frazier v. United States, 335 U.S. 497, 514–15. See also Dennis v. United States, 339 U.S. 162, 173 (opinion concurring in the result).
[28] Krulewitch v. United States, 336 U.S. 440.   [29] Id. at 445–58.
[30] Id. at 454.

The other case was *Gordon v. United States*.[31] There Justice Jackson wrote an opinion for the Court reversing a federal conviction because the trial judge had refused to compel the prosecutor to make available to the defense documents that might have been useful to impeach a prosecution witness. I am sure neither Justice Jackson nor anybody else considered *Gordon* a very important case. But in the light of his *Gordon* opinion, there is room for considerable amazement at the public outcry that followed in the wake of the *Jencks* case, decided almost three years after Justice Jackson's death.[32]

It is clear that Justice Jackson found in the Supreme Court's supervisory role over the federal judicial system a legitimate opportunity for the Court and its Justices to create and develop increasingly exacting standards in the administration of federal law. It is equally clear, I think, that no Justice was more imaginative or more demanding in the performance of that task than he was. For him this must have been a most rewarding part of the Court's work, because for him this was at the very center of the Court's most affirmative mission. His decisions in these federal cases make clear that the constraint he felt in reviewing state criminal cases under the Due Process Clause stemmed not from any lack of sensitivity on his part, but rather from his more compelling sensitivity to what he understood was his constitutional duty.

In his understanding of the Court's duty under the Due Process Clause, Justice Jackson was unable to accept either of the two theories that enabled some of his colleagues to take an "activist" position in cases arising under the Fourteenth Amendment.

[31] 344 U.S. 414.   [32] Jencks v. United States, 353 U.S. 657.

Shortly before Justice Jackson came to the Court, some of its then more junior members had embraced the comforting theory that the Fourteenth Amendment's substantive impact upon the states could be exactly measured by the specific restrictions that the first eight Amendments imposed upon the National Government.[33] I call this a "comforting" theory, because, for critics of the old Court's subjective approach to due process, it was a theory that appeared to give the Fourteenth Amendment objective content and definable scope.[34] But it was a theory that Justice Jackson was unable to accept—as constitutional history, as constitutional philosophy, or as constitutional law.[35] In the milk case from New York he bluntly recorded the simple historic fact that "the Bill of Rights Amendments were framed only as a limitation upon the powers of Congress." [36] And he was unable to find in either the words or the history of the Fourteenth Amendment any convincing evidence that its purpose or result had been to "incorporate" the first eight Amendments as restrictions upon the separate States.

He did not give full expression to these views until more than ten years after he came to the Court—in the *Beauhar-*

[33] See Adamson v. California, 332 U.S. 46, 68 (dissenting opinion of Mr. Justice Black).

[34] This theory does indeed provide limitations upon the scope of judicial review under the Fourteenth Amendment. See, e.g., the dissenting opinions of Mr. Justice Black in Griswold v. Connecticut, 381 U.S. 479, 507; Harper v. Virginia Bd. of Elections, 383 U.S. 663, 670; Berger v. New York, 388 U.S. 41, 70.

[35] In the Fourth Amendment area, e.g., compare Harris v. United States, 331 U.S. 145, 195 (dissenting opinion); United States v. Di Re. 332 U.S. 581; Johnson v. United States, 333 U.S. 10, with Irvine v. California, 347 U.S. 128.

[36] Hood & Sons v. Du Mond, 336 U.S. 525, 534.

nais case from Illinois.[37] In that case the petitioners had been convicted under an Illinois "group libel" statute for circulating an obnoxious leaflet attacking the Negro race. Justice Jackson dissented from the affirmance of the conviction, but he did so in a highly individualized separate opinion, in which he concluded, in accord with his understanding of the views of Brandeis and Holmes, that not even the First Amendment is fully "incorporated" in the Fourteenth. For him, the vast difference in the constitutional functions and concerns of the federal and state governments was decisive. He said this:

Adoption of the incorporation theory today would lead to the dilemma of either confining the States as closely as the Congress or giving the Federal Government the latitude appropriate to state governments. . . . The inappropriateness of a single standard for restricting State and Nation is indicated by the disparity between their functions and duties in relation to those freedoms. Criminality of defamation is predicated upon power either to protect the private right to enjoy integrity of reputation or the public right to tranquillity. Neither of these are objects of federal cognizance. . . .[38]

But if Justice Jackson was unable to accept the "incorporation" theory of the Fourteenth Amendment, he was even more leery of the notion that the Due Process Clause confers a roving commission to impose upon the States the Justices' own ideas of good or bad policy. This, after all, had been the very name of the game of the old Court—the whole point of the story he had told in *The Struggle for Judicial Supremacy*.

If just one opinion could be chosen to illustrate the total-

---

[37] Beauharnais v. Illinois, 343 U.S. 250.   [38] 343 U.S., at 294.

ity of his due process beliefs, it would, I think, have to be the opinion he wrote for the Court in the case of *Fay v. New York*.[39] In that case the Court rejected a Fourteenth Amendment attack upon the "blue ribbon" jury system then in use in this city and county. It is a long opinion, but these are a few of the things he had to say:

[The petitioners'] objections may well . . . warrant a political or social judgment that this special panel . . . was "unnecessary and undesirable" and that the Legislature should abolish it. But it is quite another matter to say that this Federal Court has a mandate from the Constitution to disable the special jury by setting aside its convictions. [There is a] great disparity between a legislative policy or a political judgment on the one hand and a constitutional or legal judgment on the other.[40]

The function of this federal Court under the Fourteenth Amendment in reference to state juries is not to prescribe procedures but is essentially to protect the integrity of the trial process by whatever method the state sees fit to employ. No device, whether conventional or newly devised, can be set up by which the judicial process is reduced to a sham and courts are organized to convict. They must be organized to hear, try and determine on the evidence and the law. But beyond requiring conformity to standards of fundamental fairness that have won legal recognition, this Court always has been careful not so to interpret this Amendment as to impose uniform procedures upon the several states whose legal systems stem from diverse sources of law and reflect different historical influences.

We adhere to this policy of self-restraint and will not use this great centralizing Amendment to standardize administration of justice and stagnate local variations in practice.[41]

[39] 332 U.S. 261.   [40] 332 U.S., at 281.
[41] 332 U.S., at 294–95.

Well has it been said of our power to limit state action that "To stay experimentation in things social and economic is a grave responsibility. Denial of the right to experiment may be fraught with serious consequences to the Nation. It is one of the happy incidents of the federal system that a single courageous State may, if its citizens choose, serve as a laboratory; and try novel social and economic experiments without risk to the rest of the country." [42]

These final words were the famous words of Mr. Justice Brandeis.

For Justice Jackson the true function of the Fourteenth Amendment's Due Process Clause in state criminal cases was, as he put it in the blue ribbon jury case, to assure that courts are organized not "to convict" but "to hear, try and determine on the evidence and the law." [43] Two cases, I think, clearly illustrate his meaning. One was a case from Florida, in which he, unlike seven of his colleagues, would have reversed a rape conviction of two Negroes because he thought the integrity of their trial had been totally undermined by inflammatory newspaper publicity.[44] The other was a case from Pennsylvania, where a prison sentence had been imposed by a trial judge who had been falsely informed about the defendant's previous criminal record. In that case Justice Jackson wrote a Court opinion setting aside the judgment under the Due Process Clause.[45]

Justice Jackson's fundamental beliefs about the necessary limits of the Court's function under the Due Process Clause were elaborated in many cases, often in dissent.

[42] 332 U.S., at 296.   [43] 332 U.S., at 294.
[44] Shepherd v. Florida, 341 U.S. 50 (concurring opinion). The Court reversed on other grounds.
See also Craig v. Harney, 331 U.S. 367, 394 (dissenting opinion).
[45] Townsend v. Burke, 334 U.S. 736.

When, in a case from Tennessee,[46] the Court reversed the conviction of a man for the murder of his wife because of the way in which a confession had been obtained, his dissenting opinion was not only forceful, but somewhat prophetic:

We must bear in mind that this case does not come here from a lower federal court over whose conduct we may assert a general supervisory power. If it did, we should be at liberty to apply rules as to the admissibility of confessions, based on our own conception of permissible procedure. . . . We may not lay down rules of evidence for [the state courts] nor revise their decisions merely because we feel more confidence in our own wisdom and rectitude. . . .

The burden of protecting society from most crimes against persons and property falls upon the State. Different States have different crime problems and some freedom to vary procedures according to their own ideas. Here a State was forced by an unwitnessed and baffling murder to vindicate its law and protect its society. To . . . divine in the due process clause of the Fourteenth Amendment an exclusion of confessions on an irrebuttable presumption that custody and examination are "inherently coercive" . . . requires us to make more than a passing expression of our doubts and disagreements.[47]

Questioning is an indispensable instrumentality of justice. . . . [W]e cannot read an undiscriminating hostility to mere interrogation into the Constitution without unduly fettering the States in protecting society from the criminal.[48]

[D]oes the Constitution prohibit use of all confessions made after arrest because questioning, while one is deprived of

---

[46] Ashcraft v. Tennessee, 322 U.S. 143. See also Watts v. Indiana. 338 U.S. 49, 57 (separate opinion); Gallegos v. Nebraska, 342 U.S. 55, 68 (concurring opinion); Stein v. New York, 346 U.S. 156.

[47] 322 U.S., at 158–59.   [48] 322 U.S., at 160.

freedom, is "inherently coercive"? The Court does not quite say so, but it is moving far and fast in that direction.[49]

The use of the due process clause to disable the States in protection of society from crime is quite as dangerous and delicate a use of federal judicial power as to use it to disable them from social or economic experimentation. . . .[50]

In another case Justice Jackson protested the use of the Due Process Clause to upset what he thought were valid criminal convictions in the state courts through the writ of federal habeas corpus. I repeat here only a little of what he had to say:

Rightly or wrongly, the belief is widely held by the practicing profession that this Court no longer respects impersonal rules of law but is guided in these matters by personal impressions which from time to time may be shared by a majority of Justices. Whatever has been intended, this Court also has generated an impression in much of the judiciary that regard for precedents and authorities is obsolete, that words no longer mean what they have always meant to the profession, that the law knows no fixed principles.[51]

[49] 322 U.S., at 161.

[50] 322 U.S., at 174. Justice Jackson continued:
"The warning words of Mr. Justice Holmes in his dissenting opinion in Baldwin v. Missouri . . . seem . . . appropriate for rereading now."
  Those "warning words" were:
"I have not yet adequately expressed the more than anxiety that I feel at the ever increasing scope given to the Fourteenth Amendment in cutting down what I believe to be the constitutional rights of the States. As the decisions now stand, I see hardly any limit but the sky to the invalidating of those rights if they happen to strike a majority of this Court as for any reason undesirable. I cannot believe that the Amendment was intended to give us *carte blanche* to embody our economic or moral beliefs in its prohibitions. . . ." Baldwin v. Missouri, 281 U.S. 586, 595 (dissenting opinion of Mr. Justice Holmes).

[51] Brown v. Allen, 344 U.S. 443, 535 (opinion concurring in the result).

[R]eversal by a higher court is not proof that justice is thereby better done. There is no doubt that if there were a super-Supreme Court, a substantial proportion of our reversals of state courts would also be reversed. We are not final because we are infallible, but we are infallible only because we are final.[52]

These, then, were the contours of Justice Jackson's beliefs about the legitimate balance of state and federal power under the Due Process Clause of the Fourteenth Amendment. What was the foundation for these beliefs, and what was their motivation? A large part of the answer to that question is transparently clear. As a constitutional lawyer, he simply could not find in the Due Process Clause any warrant for the Court to impose its own abstract views of wisdom or justice upon the legislatures or courts of the States. He thought the old Court had been tragically wrong in presuming to do so, and he could not bring himself to believe that it was any less wrong on the part of contemporary Justices, regardless of how thoroughly he might have personally shared their political or moral views. The members of the old Court, Justice Jackson never forgot, were also righteous and sincere and patriotic men. And they, too, had announced their decisions in the name of individual freedom.

It is not much of a test of constitutional principle, I think he would have said, for a Justice to exercise restraint in dealing with a state law or practice that he personally approves. The test comes with a state law or practice that a Justice personally thinks is unwise or even wrong. Justice Jackson met that test with resolute self-discipline. I need only remind you again of his opinion in the federal government employee jury case under the Court's supervisory

[52] 344 U.S., at 540.

power, and his opinion in the New York blue ribbon jury case under the Due Process Clause. In the one case he was free to give rein to his own views of wise policy. In the other he knew it was his duty *not* to impose his own views on the State of New York in the name of the Fourteenth Amendment.

Throughout his judicial career Justice Jackson remained the despair of those Court observers—and they are many—who fatuously insist on pinning a "conservative" or "liberal" label on every Justice. To the result-oriented critics of the Court—and they are far too many—he remained something of a puzzle to the end.[53] I think he would have regarded their puzzlement with detachment, if not with scorn. For he would have remembered, if they did not, that neither "liberals" nor "conservatives" have had a monopoly on judicial activism.[54]

But what I have said is not, I think, the whole explanation for Justice Jackson's views about the constitutional balance of state and federal power. For him, judicial restraint was not a negative concept. It reflected his positive belief in the felicitous, if fortuitous, rightness of the basic political compromise that underlies our constitutional

[53] See *Time*, Oct. 18, 1954, "A Hard Man to Pigeonhole," p. 24.

[54] See Richard N. Goodwin, "The Shape of American Politics," Commentary, June 1967, pp. 25, 26–27:
"[T]he nine justices of the Supreme Court make major political decisions, unresponsive to the democratic process, in secret meetings on Friday afternoons. Both the number and the scope of such decisions steadily mount. Liberal critics have generally approved this development because they approve the content of the decisions, while the fundamental reshaping of an important institution seems not to trouble them. But it is a transformation which almost certainly will come back to plague us as judicial personnel and social attitudes change, and as an institution which has become more and more political develops an even greater sensitivity to transitory shifts in the political temper."

structure—a structure that recognizes and preserves the values of diversity in our national life. For him these were precious values, for he knew that in its diversity our society has found resilience, initiative, and strength.[55] When he quoted the words of Brandeis about the "happy incidents of the federal system" he was not indulging in empty rhetoric. Steeped as he was in history, he knew that the evolution of social and legal and moral progress in America has often been initiated by the enlightened and inventive action of the people of a single State—that a development like workmen's compensation, to name one example, could never have evolved as it did without the freedom of the individual States to replace the jury trial of the common law with a prompt and effective administrative proceeding.

Justice Jackson saw as clearly as the next the inevitability of a continuing thrust towards centralized power in the constitutional evolution of our Nation. And he would have been as quick as the next to condemn those who would use the banner of States' rights as a cloak for social injustice. But for these very reasons he insistently believed that in areas of legitimate state concern the way must be kept free for the processes of self-reliant democracy to work—for the people of each State to respond to their own changing needs.

He saw in the heavy hand of a national policy-making court a threat to that kind of representative self-government. He saw that "judicial activism" could be a deadening and stultifying force. He knew that every coer-

---

[55] Chief Judge Desmond has told us that one of Justice Jackson's "proud boasts about his beloved city of Jamestown was that it was 'a city where everyone is free to speak in support of any ism that he likes.' " *Ante.*

cive and centralizing court decision deals a blow, if sometimes only a little blow, first to the ability and then to the
will of the democratic process to operate with responsibility
and vigor. He understood, as only an experienced advocate
could understand, the shortcomings of the adversary process
as a substitute for the give and take of informed self-
government. He understood, as only a wise and sophisticated judge could understand, how fallible the judges of
even a final court can be. He knew that the right answer to
a problem in New York might not be the right answer in
North Dakota. He knew also that there might be no single
right answer in either State, and that there might be a better answer tomorrow than the best of today's. He knew, in
short, that the great strength of the federal union our Constitution created lies in its capacity for self-innovation and
change.

In the last of the Godkin Lectures, Justice Jackson
wrote of a "cult of libertarian judicial activists," who

believe that the Court can find in a 4,000-word eighteenth-
century document or its nineteenth-century Amendments, or
can plausibly supply, some clear bulwark against all dangers and
evils that today beset us internally. This assumes that the Court
will be the dominant factor in shaping the constitutional practice of the future and can and will maintain, not only equality
with the elective branches, but a large measure of supremacy
and control over them. I may be biased against this attitude
because it is so contrary to the doctrines of the critics of the
Court, of whom I was one, at the time of the Roosevelt proposal to reorganize the judiciary. But it seems to me a doctrine
wholly incompatible with faith in democracy, and in so far as
it encourages a belief that the judges may be left to correct

the result of public indifference to issues of liberty in choosing Presidents, Senators, and Representatives, it is a vicious teaching.[56]

That is forceful language. But the key word, I think, is "faith." Justice Jackson knew that the Framers had put their ultimate faith in the people, and there, for better or for worse, he put his faith too.[57] He firmly believed that only so long as we remain a free and responsible people can there endure a society to be truly served by the profession he loved so much and the Court he served so well.

POTTER STEWART

[56] The Supreme Court in the American System of Government, p. 58.

[57] Justice Jackson closed the last of his Godkin Lectures by quoting the words he had spoken as Attorney General upon the occasion of the 150th anniversary of the Supreme Court:

"However well the Court and its bar may discharge their tasks, the destiny of this Court is inseparably linked to the fate of our democratic system of representative government. Judicial functions, as we have evolved them, can be discharged only in that kind of society which is willing to submit its conflicts to adjudication and to subordinate power to reason. The future of the Court may depend more upon the competence of the executive and legislative branches of government to solve their problems adequately and in time than upon the merit which is its own." *Id.* pp. 82–83.

Robert H. Jackson's Contributions During the Nuremberg Trial

THE RIGHT HONORABLE LORD SHAWCROSS
With an Introduction by
WHITNEY NORTH SEYMOUR, ESQ.

In 1945, shortly before the end of the war, it was decided that the Germans responsible for the horrible war crimes in World War II should be tried for their violations of international law before an international tribunal constituted by the Americans, English, French, and Russians. President Truman, at the suggestion of our former President, Judge Rosenman, asked Mr. Justice Jackson to take leave of the Supreme Court, negotiate the agreement for the trials, and serve as the American prosecutor. He responded affirmatively to this call to duty. Several months were spent in negotiating the agreement. Lord Shawcross has said of Jackson's role in those difficult negotiations:

Mr. Justice Jackson's burning conviction that it was the duty of the United Nations to expose and punish the crimes committed by the leaders of Nazi Germany in forcing war upon the world and in the conduct of the war itself was one of the greatest single personal factors in bringing into being the London

Charter and Agreement which formed the jurisdictional basis
of the Nuremberg proceedings.

*The English Government changed while the negotia-
tions were going on but in the relatively imperturbable way
the English conduct great affairs, plans went forward steadily and only the roles of some of the participants changed.
Where Sir David Maxwell Fyfe, the Conservative Attorney
General had chaired the negotiations and was to serve as
the Chief British Prosecutor, now Lord Shawcross, then Sir
Hartley, came in as Labor Attorney General and Chief
Prosecutor with Sir David as Chief Assistant.*

*I will not make reference here to the trial, which Lord
Shawcross will cover in his usual spirited way. I would
merely like to quote Lord Birkett's comments about Bob
Jackson's advocacy at the trial, from his introduction to
Eugene Gerhart's life of Jackson:*

In the court itself, sitting as I did on the Bench day by day,
I had the opportunity of seeing a superb exhibition of advocacy,
notably in the opening speech when he outlined the case for
the prosecution in most memorable and striking language, and
in the closing speech when, after many, many months of evidence, he made the most masterly summing-up of "as vast and
varied a panorama of events as ever has been compressed within
the framework of a litigation," to use his own description.
These two speeches have been singled out by lawyers all over
the world as supreme examples of advocacy, and I will therefore
only add this word. One of the marks of the highest advocacy
has always been the ability to make an orderly presentation to
the court of the most complicated facts, but it is safe to say that
never in the history of criminal trials was so complicated a case
ever set before counsel, and never did any counsel emerge from

it so triumphantly. These two great speeches, in my opinion, are the superb triumphs of his days at Nuremberg.

One naturally has some questions as we look back at Nuremberg. Dealing with Justice Jackson, was it wise for the President to draft a Supreme Court Justice for that task? Did his absence at Nuremberg deprive him of the Chief Justiceship when Chief Justice Stone died in 1946? And then in a wider view, did the judgments at Nuremberg advance the rule of law by demonstrating that conduct which affronts the conscience of mankind will sometimes be punished? I suppose each of us would have his own answers and we shall be interested to see whether Lord Shawcross's lecture aids in providing answers. My own would be that it would be wise if Presidents restrained the natural impulse to turn to the Supreme Court for help in great emergencies, and refrain from making calls on the patriotism of the Justices which it is almost impossible to resist. In the long run it will be better not to ask Supreme Court Justices to step out of their roles. We probably lost a great Chief Justice because Jackson patriotically yielded to the call to service. On balance, Nuremberg did advance the rule of law because it showed that the conscience of mankind is not always asleep and that man's inhumanity to man does not always go upunished.

Lord Shawcross is so familiar a friend that it would be an act of supererogation to introduce him to any American legal audience. He has been one of our honorary members since 1946. He was a great Chairman of the English Bar Council and an outstanding Attorney General. I have heard it said that he was without peer as a barrister arguing *a complicated case. After his retirement from the bar, he served as director of Shell, and on his retirement from that became adviser to important English and American interests. Somehow conservatism has made an increasing appeal to him in recent years, but in whatever group he is found, his is likely to be the most interesting and well-informed voice. I am sure he believes as we all do, that in a dangerous world nothing must be allowed to sever the hoops of steel and the golden cords of friendship that bind together England and America, and especially the legal professions.*

WHITNEY NORTH SEYMOUR, ESQ.

———————

Others are more competent to pass upon the contribution which the late Justice Robert H. Jackson made to the life of this country, whether in the field of advocacy, playing his part as a country lawyer and a member of this Association in the integrity of legal administration, whether as Attorney General of the United States, a politician and a statesman, or as a courageous and farsighted member of that renowned institution, the Supreme Court of the United States. I know his contribution to have been a great one. But in spite of all the disillusion of this last score of years, I am still optimistic enough to think that in the pages of history, Justice Jackson will best be remembered for the leading part he played in promoting the growth of international law through the process at Nuremberg. That, indeed, would have been his own wish. "The hard months at Nuremberg were well spent in the most important, enduring, and constructive work of my life," [1] he once wrote.

[1] Whitney Harris, *Tyranny on Trial*, Southern Methodist University Press, 1954.

We at the Bar in England have a practice not to make speeches about the cases in which we have been concerned. And, apart from one speech at the Assembly of the United Nations, I have not hitherto spoken about Nuremberg. But the Nuremberg process was altogether exceptional and I regard it as a great privilege to have been asked to speak about it here in tribute to my old friend, my colleague in those proceedings.

It is not that Justice Jackson was the originator of the proposal that there should be a judicial trial of the war criminals or that he shared the responsibility for the policy decision that such a trial should be held, although it is true that his public statements influenced it. Those were matters which came before his own involvement. It is that the decision to hold such a trial having been taken as a matter of policy, its fulfillment and success depended more upon the wisdom, the vision, the organizational capacity, and the leadership of Justice Jackson than upon anything else.

But perhaps one should begin at the beginning. And in what I shall say I have had the very great assistance in matters of fact (although he has no responsibility for expressions of opinion) of one of my country's leading historians, Sir John Wheeler-Bennett, who was himself attached to the United Kingdom team at Nuremberg. It was, I think, in October 1941, while the United States was still neutral, that President Roosevelt drew attention to the wholesale execution of French hostages. "One day", he said, "a frightful retribution would be exacted." [2]

I am not sure that up to that time the British had made any pronouncement upon the matter: we had been too fully involved in our own struggle for survival to bother

[2] David Kilmuir, *Political Adventure*, London, 1964, p. 78.

much about what we would do to our enemies when we won. As Mr. Secretary Stimson was to write later: "We did not ask ourselves in 1939 or in 1940 or even in 1941 what punishment if any Hitler and his chief assistants deserved." [3] But in August 1942 President Roosevelt solemnly warned the Axis Powers that "the time will come when they will have to stand in the Courts of Law in the very countries they were oppressing and answer for their acts." [4] And in October of that year in the United Kingdom a Committee was formed under the chairmanship of the Lord Chancellor to consider the problem of war criminals in all its aspects and to decide what steps should be taken preparatory to inter-allied agreement as to the course to be adopted. At the end of 1942, the Committee directed that the Treasury Solicitor should be charged with the task of collecting material upon which charges might subsequently be laid. But the matter first arose for inter-allied discussion and agreement in October 1943, at the Moscow Conference of Foreign Ministers. Mr. Cordell Hull expressed a forthright opinion: "If I had my way," he said, "I would take Hitler and Mussolini and Tojo and their accomplices and bring them before a drumhead Court Martial and at sunrise on the following morning there would occur an historic incident."

Mr. Molotov too was, perhaps, less unexpectedly in favor of "stern swift justice." The British position was equivocal and before the matter was finally settled it changed completely. On this occasion, Mr. Eden is recorded as saying that all the legal forms should be observed.[5] What he

[3] Henry L. Stimson, "The Nuremberg Trial," *Foreign Affairs*, January, 1947.

[4] *New York Times*, August 22, 1942.

[5] Cordell Hull, *Memoirs*, II., 1289-90.

meant by that I am not sure. The following month, the Big Three, Roosevelt, Churchill, and Stalin met at Teheran. It was their first meeting: there were many other matters to discuss and it was not until the final dinner party on November 29th that the question of the war criminals came to be discussed. It was an unfortunate atmosphere. Marshal Stalin said that at least 500,000 of the German General Staff must be physically and summarily liquidated. President Roosevelt, perhaps regarding this suggestion as having been put forward in jest, however grim, countered it in that spirit by saying that it should only be 49,000. But Winston Churchill does not seem to have thought the subject a matter for humor. He was shocked: he said that the British would never stand for such mass murders. "I would rather", he said, "be taken out into the garden here and now and be shot myself than sully my own and my country's honour with such infamy." [6] In the end, the actual Communique, or Moscow Declaration as it was called, left the matter somewhat in the air. Those Nazis who had been responsible for or had taken an active part in atrocities, massacres, and executions would be sent back to the countries in which their abominable deeds were done in order that they might be judged and punished according to the laws of those liberated countries and of the free Governments which will be created therein. Major criminals, it was added, whose offenses had no particular geographical location, would be punished by the joint decision of the Governments of the Allies. This sounds like executive action but in fact the question whether to have a trial, and for what crimes, remained open and was the subject of much debate.

[6] Charles Bohlen, Minutes of Conferences at Cairo and Teheran, p. 553.

Of course, 1944 was a year in which the United States and England were preoccupied with building up the immense effort which was to win the war. But in the early autumn of that year, Mr. Stimson, the Secretary for War, and a distinguished member of the New York Bar, delegated the planning of the matter to Mr. John McCloy, the Assistant Secretary. In a Memorandum of September 9th, 1944, Mr. Stimson wrote:

The other fundamental point upon which I feel we differ is the matter of the trial and punishment of those Germans who are responsible for crimes and depredations. Under the plan proposed by Mr. Morgenthau, the so-called archcriminals shall be put to death by the military without provision for any trial and upon mere identification after apprehension. The method of dealing with these and other criminals requires careful thought and a well-defined procedure. Such procedure must embody, in my judgment, at least the rudimentary aspects of the Bill of Rights, namely, notification to the accused of the charge, the right to be heard and, within reasonable limits, to call witnesses in his defense.[7]

At the Quebec Conference in that year, the question of judicial trial as against executive shooting was not decided, but Mr. Stimson is said to have heard from Mr. McCloy reports that the President had there expressed himself as definitely in favor of execution without trial:

It seemed probably a curbstone opinion but it was deeply disturbing to the War Department and Stimson and McCloy promptly set up a group of military lawyers to study in detail the possibilities for a trial. After a month of study these lawyers reported to the Secretary. . . . (they) had reached the conclusion that besides local tribunals to punish war crimes against the

[7] Henry L. Stimson, *On Active Service*, p. 584.

international rules of war, we could for the same purpose establish an International Tribunal if we wished it or mixed Tribunals, the latter to prosecute criminals whose criminal activities had extended over several jurisdictions. . . . Colonel Bernays of the J.A.G.D. gave an interesting talk on the possibility of bringing charges against the whole scheme of Nazi totalitarian war, using for the promotion of its end methods of warfare which were in conflict with the established rules of war. This was virtually upon the theory of a conspiracy. . . ." [8]

Mr. Stimson was much attracted by the concept of a conspiracy as being the guide to a proper course in trying the Nazi leaders, and he reported on it to the President:

I told him the story of the 17 holes—the case I tried against the American Sugar Refining Corporation. He was greatly interested in this and gave his very frank approval to my suggestion when I said that conspiracy . . . with . . . representatives of all classes of actors brought in from top to bottom would be the best way to try it and would give us a record and also a trial which would certainly persuade any onlooker of the evil of the Nazi system. [9]

The President was already shifting from his position and he appointed Judge Roseman, his personal Counsel, to study the problem. In January, 1945, the Secretaries of State and War and the Attorney General submitted a detailed Memorandum setting out a carefully reasoned argument in favor of a judicial trial on charges of conspiracy:

The German leaders and the organizations employed by them, such as those referred to above (SA. SS., Gestapo), should be charged both with the commission of their atrocious crimes, and also with joint participation in a broad criminal enterprise

[8] *Ibid.*, Oct. 24, 1944.   [9] *Ibid.*, p. 586.

which included and intended these crimes, or was reasonably calculated to bring them about. The allegation of the criminal enterprise would be so couched as to permit full proof of the entire Nazi plan from its inception and the means used in its furtherance and execution, including the prewar atrocities and those committed against their own nationals, neutrals, and stateless persons, as well as the waging of an illegal war of aggression with ruthless disregard for international law and the rules of war. Such a charge would be firmly founded upon the rule of liability, common to all penal systems and included in the general doctrines of the laws of war, that those who participate in the formulation and execution of a criminal plan involving multiple crimes are jointly liable for each of the offenses committed and jointly responsible for the acts of each other. Under such a charge there are admissible in evidence the acts of any of the conspirators done in furtherance of the conspiracy, whether or not these acts were in themselves criminal and subject to separate prosecution as such.[10]

This was the so-called Yalta Memorandum, but at the Yalta Conference no action was taken other than an agreement for later consideration by the Governments there represented.

Accordingly, the President sent Judge Rosenman to Europe to conduct negotiations with the Governments concerned. The British Government was opposed to the proposal of a judicial trial, and on the very day President Roosevelt died, the British War Cabinet passed a resolution in favor of "executive action." Judge Rosenman records in a recent letter that after he returned to London (where he was assisted by Judge Cutter and General Weir) he had:

[10] Report of Robert H. Jackson, London 1945, Department of State Publication 3080, p. 6.

Long separate talks with the Prime Minister (including a weekend at Chequers), the Lord Chancellor, Anthony Eden and others of the British War Cabinet. With all of them I repeated what President Roosevelt had said to me, namely that in order to establish documentary proof of all that the Nazis had done and to prevent the rise of a new Napoleonic myth a trial should be held before an International Tribunal. All of these individuals as well as the British War Cabinet itself, stated in no uncertain terms that they wanted to treat the top six or seven Nazi criminals in a political military manner, namely to execute them and to announce to the world the next morning that they had been shot.

In fact the very day that President Roosevelt died, the British War Cabinet held a special meeting and again decided formally that they favored this kind of disposal of the top Nazis. In my conference with them, there was always the precedent of the way Napoleon was treated after defeat except that he was not shot but was exiled without any trial.[11]

President Truman was not slow to endorse his predecessor's instructions that there must be a trial. Justice Jackson had written an article in the *Atlantic Monthly* setting forth the scope and importance of such a trial, and President Truman told Judge Rosenman that he proposed to appoint Jackson at once as Chief of Counsel before an International Tribunal. On May 2nd, Justice Jackson's appointment was announced. He did not resign from the Court but in effect was suspended from active participation in its membership until his new task should be complete. It seems to have been expected at that time that he would have been back by October, and some cases on which the Court was decided were adjourned pending his return.[12]

11 Letter to Judge Cutter, 15.6.67.
12 Report of Mr. Justice Jackson, U. S. State Publication 3080, p. 212.

There was, of course, some criticism of the appointment by those who thought that a Judge of the Supreme Court of the United States should not step down into the arena, whether of political affairs or of the trial as distinct from the adjudication of cases. There were comments in the newspapers, and some of his colleagues on the Bench disapproved of Jackson's acceptance of the appointment. Thus, according to Justice Felix Frankfurter, Justice Harlan Stone "beefed about (a man leaving the Supreme Court to do a political job) a lot. You know a man on the Supreme Court should never do anything else." [13] Indeed, Justice Stone, whether because he disliked the idea of Jackson taking time off from the Court or not, disapproved of the whole exercise and wrote about "Jackson's lynching expedition." [14] It was nothing of the kind: the circumstances were altogether exceptional, and the appointment of a Supreme Court Judge certainly not political in any narrow sense—certainly less so than the appointment of Justice Goldberg to the United Nations. Here was the task of representing his country at an International Tribunal of historic importance which was to decide not on political grounds but judicially issues of momentous importance to mankind. Justice Jackson did not hesitate as to where his duty lay.

And so, at the beginning of May, he was plunged into this great project, the nature of which had been settled as a matter of principle by his own Government but had by no means been agreed to by the other Allies and the actual carrying out of which presented the most formidable difficulties. It is not to belittle the great importance of his dominant

[13] Felix Frankfurter, *Felix Frankfurter Reminisces*, London, 1960, p. 222.
[14] Francis Biddle, *In Brief Authority*, New York, 1962, p. 375.

position at the trial itself to say that the two tasks of re-
search into and preparation of the case itself, and the negotiations of an agreement as to the form and method of
Trial, were at once the most difficult and the most important of Justice Jackson's contribution to the whole project.
The British remained hostile to the idea of a trial. Only a
week before Jackson had been brought into the matter, the
British Government had submitted to Judge Rosenman an
Aide Memoire which set out their view strongly against a
judicial trial and in favor of "executive action." It is worth
quoting:

1. H.M.G. assume that it is beyond question that Hitler and
a number of arch-criminals associated with him (including
Mussolini) must, so far as they fall into Allied hands, suffer
the penalty of death for their conduct leading up to the war
and for the wickedness which they have either themselves
perpetrated or have authorized in the conduct of the war. It
would be manifestly impossible to punish war criminals of a
lower grade by a capital sentence pronounced by a Military
Court unless the ringleaders are dealt with equal severity. This
is really involved in the concluding sentence of the Moscow
Declaration on this subject, which reserves for the arch-criminals whose offences have no special localization treatment to
be determined in due course by the Allies.

2. It being conceded that these leaders must suffer death,
the question arises whether they should be tried by some form
of tribunal claiming to exercise judicial functions, or whether
the decision taken by the Allies should be reached and enforced
without the machinery of a trial. H.M.G. thoroughly appreciate the arguments which have been advanced in favour of some
form of preliminary trial. But H.M.G. are also deeply impressed
with the dangers and difficulties of this course, and they wish
to put before their principal Allies, in a connected form, the

arguments which have led them to think that execution without trial is the preferable course.

3. The central consideration for deciding this difficult choice must, in H.M.G.'s view, be reached by asking—what is the real charge which the Allied people and the world as a whole makes against Hitler? It is the totality of his offences against the international standard which civilised countries try to observe which makes him the scoundrel that he is. If he were to be indicted for these offences in the manner that is necessary for reasons of justice in a criminal court, and if his fate is to be determined on the conclusion reached by the tribunal as to the truth of this bundle of charges and the adequacy of the proof, it seems impossible to conceive that the trial would not be exceedingly long and elaborate. He, of course, must have in such a trial all the rights properly conceded to an accused person. He must be defended, if he wishes, by counsel, and he must call any relevant evidence. According to British ideas, at any rate, his defence could not be forcibly shut down or limited because it involves a great expenditure of time. There is nothing upon which British opinion is more sensitive in the realm of criminal procedure than the suspicion that an accused person—whatever the depths of his crime—has been denied his full defense.

4. There is a further consideration which, in the view of H.M.G., needs to be very carefully weighed. If the method of public trial were adopted, the comment must be expected from the very start to be that the whole thing is a "put-up-job" designed by the Allies to justify a punishment they have already resolved on. Hitler and his advisers—if they decide to take part and to challenge what is alleged—may be expected to be very much alive to any opportunity of turning the tables. Public opinion as the trial goes on is likely to weary at the length of the process. It is difficult to think that anybody would in the course of time look on Hitler as an injured man, but it is by no means unlikely that a long trial will result in a change of public feeling as to the justification of trying Hitler at all.

Will not some people begin to say, "The man should be shot out of hand?" And if in the complicated and novel procedure which such a trial is bound to adopt—for Russian, American and British ideas must in some way be amalgamated—the defence secured some unexpected point, is there not a danger of the trial being denounced as a farce?

5. There is a further point. Reference has been made above to Hitler's conduct leading up to the war as one of the crimes on which the Allies would rely. There should be included in this the unprovoked attacks which, since the original declaration of war, he has made on various countries. These are not war crimes in the ordinary sense, nor is it at all clear that they can properly be described as crimes under international law. These would, however, necessarily have to be part of the charge and if the tribunal had—as presumably they would have—to proceed according to international law, an argument, which might be a formidable argument, would be open to the accused that this part of the indictment should be struck out. It may well be thought by some that these acts ought to be regarded as crimes under international law. Under the procedure suggested this would be a matter for the tribunal, and would at any rate give the accused the opportunity of basing arguments on what has happened in the past and what has been done by various countries in declaring war which resulted in acquiring new territory, which certainly were not regarded at the time as crimes against international law.

6. H.M.G. earnestly hope that their Allies will consider the arguments set out above for they are most anxious that a very early agreement should be reached as to the methods of dealing with Hitler and his chief associates, and that the method should be one in which the principal Allies concur. It would in any case be valuable if a document could now be drawn up giving the reasoned basis for the punishment of the men concerned.[15]

15 Report of Mr. Justice Jackson, Department of State Publication 3080, p. 18.

The President's overt reply to that had been the appointment of Justice Jackson himself. The San Francisco Conference of the United Nations was imminent. Immediately
after President Roosevelt's death, Judge Rosenman returned to Washington and in conference with Justice Jackson and representatives of the State, the War and the Justice Departments, a plan was drawn up providing for an
executive agreement between the Four Great Powers to
implement the Yalta principles and establish a Military
Tribunal. The Memorandum accompanying the suggested
Executive Agreement explicitly stated that the German
leaders, additionally to be charged with specific atrocities,
should be indicted for their joint participation in a broad
criminal enterprise, thus permitting full proof of the Nazi
plan from its inception and involving the organizations, like
the S.S., upon which the Nazi system rested. These were
historic documents, for after months of argument and controversy they formed the basis of the eventual agreement
and charter upon which the International Military Tribunal
at Nuremberg was founded. Some minor changes were made
in the drafts at San Francisco and they were delivered to
the Foreign Ministers of Russia, France, and Britain. There
were some informal discussions and the British Government seems to have resiled from the position set out in its
Note of April 23rd. There was now acceptance in principle
of the policy of establishing an International Military
Tribunal to try the major criminals and a decision to set up
at once a Committee of Chiefs of Counsel representing
each of the four Governments to prepare and manage the
Prosecutions. Justice Jackson proceeded to gather his team
around him: he selected men from the different Services
and Departments involved, often but not always lawyers,

took over the control of the measures already in hand for collecting and sifting the evidence, and generally put into motion all the immense activity which was to be required for the preparation of the main case. But there was still lacking any formal agreement that there should be a main case, how or where it was to be conducted, and what the charges should be. As he said later, he was so impressed with the immensity of the task that he thought it unwise to wait for the completion of international arrangements before commencing the preparation of the American case.[16]

On May 22nd Jackson went to Europe. He went to Paris, to Frankfurt, to Wiesbaden, to London. He had innumerable and extended conferences with all concerned— General Eisenhower in Paris, the Lord Chancellor and Foreign Secretary Eden in London, and with representatives of the French Provisional Government. On June 6th he was able to report that the British and French Governments accepted the United States proposals in principle and that the Soviet Government, while not committed, was thought likely to unite in the prosecution. This Report to the President was a remarkable document: within 5 weeks of his appointment, Justice Jackson had set up the administrative machinery which was required, had formulated the general principles on which the charges to be laid against the leading Nazis should be based, and had set out the manner in which he thought those charges could fairly and judicially be brought to trial. Let me cite just two passages from this notable Report:

The American case is being prepared on the assumption that an inescapable responsibility rests upon this country to conduct an inquiry, preferably in association with others, but alone if

16 *Ibid.*, p. 18.

necessary, into the culpability of those whom there is probable cause to accuse of atrocities and other crimes. We have many such men in our possession. What shall we do with them? We could, of course, set them at large without a hearing. But it has cost unmeasured thousands of American lives to beat and bind these men. To free them without a trial would mock the dead and make cynics of the living. On the other hand, we could execute or otherwise punish them without a hearing. But undiscriminating executions or punishments without definite findings of guilt, fairly arrived at, would violate pledges repeatedly given, and would not set easily on the American conscience or be remembered by our children with pride. The only other course is to determine the innocence or guilt of the accused after a hearing as dispassionate as the times and horrors we deal with will permit, and upon a record that will leave our reasons and motives clear.

Because I, too, feel a sense of urgency, I have proceeded with the preparations of the American case before completion of the diplomatic exchanges concerning the Tribunal to hear it and the agreement under which we are to work. We must, however, recognize the existence of serious difficulties to be overcome in preparation of the case. It is no criticism to say that until the surrender of Germany the primary objective of the military intelligence services was naturally to gather military information rather than to prepare a legal case for trial. We must now sift and compress within a workable scope voluminous evidence relating to a multitude of crimes committed in several countries and participated in by thousands of actors over a decade of time. The preparation must cover military, naval, diplomatic, political, and commercial aggressions. The evidence is scattered among various agencies and in the hands of several armies. The captured documentary evidence—literally tons of orders, records and reports—is largely in foreign languages. Every document and the trial itself must be rendered into several languages. An immense amount of work is necessary to bring this evidence together physically, to select what is useful, to integrate it into a case, to overlook no relevant detail, and at the same time and at all costs to avoid becoming lost in a wilderness of single instances. Some sacrifice of perfection to speed can wisely be made and, of course, urgency overrides every personal convenience and comfort for all of us who are engaged in this work.[17]

By early in June the matter had so far progressed that the British Government suggested that representatives of the four Governments should meet in conference in London. The Conference commenced on June 26th, but in the meantime the Soviet Government had indicated that while agreeing in general with the American proposal for a joint trial of the "leaders of the Hitlerite Government," they had very different ideas both as to the charges and to the procedure. It could in any event, have been no easy task. There was the problem of three different languages. Still more, of three, if not four, entirely different systems of law, each with its own technical vocabulary and each having its own principles and its distinct procedures. As the meetings of the London Conference dragged on, it became apparent that there were differences not of detail but of philosophy.

Thus Justice Jackson:

I think we are in a philosophical difference that lies at the root of a great many technical differences and will continue to lie at the root of differences unless we can reconcile our basic viewpoints. As the statement of our Soviet colleague said, they proceed on the assumption that the declarations of Crimea and Moscow already convict these parties and that the charges need not be tried before independent judges empowered to render an

[17] *Ibid.*

independent decision on guilt. Now that underlies a great deal of their position, and we don't make that assumption. In the first place, the President of the United States has no power to convict anybody. He can only accuse. He can not arrest in most cases without judicial authority. Therefore, the accusation made carries no weight in an American trial whatever. These declarations are an accusation and not a conviction. That requires a judicial finding. Now we could not be parties to setting up a more formal judicial body to ratify a political decision to convict. The judges will have to inquire into the evidence and reach an independent decision. There is a great deal of realism in Mr. Nikitchenko's statement. There could be but one decision in this case—that we are bound to concede. But the reason is the evidence and not the statements made by heads of state with reference to these cases. That is the reason why, at the very beginning, the position of the United States was that there must be trials rather than political executions. The United States feels we could not make political executions. I took that position publicly. I have no sympathy with these men, but, if we are going to have a trial, then it must be an actual trial. That is the position of the American Government, and it troubles me a bit to think of trying to solve by a subcommittee so fundamental a disagreement as to trial. It raises the question of whether procedural differences are not so great that the idea of separate tribunals for each nation for the trial of its separate groups of prisoners may not be the easiest and most satisfactory way of reconciling it. I do not know, but just put that forward."

General Nikitchenko:

Perhaps I am mistaken, but I understand that our purpose is not to discuss the philosophy of law but to try and work out an agreement, the purpose of which would be the carrying on of justice in the naming of the war criminals. . . ." [18]

[18] International Conference on Military Tribunals, Document XVII.

Quite early, Justice Jackson had to make it clear—and this was no idle threat—that if need be the United States would have to "go it alone" as the modern jargon has it. In a Memorandum on the 30th June, Jackson said:

I call attention to the official statement of the responsibility which the United States conceives it has for the trial of prisoners in its possession as outlined in my report to the President, a copy of which we have provided. By reason of the President's unqualified endorsement of it, the essentials it states represent the President's view as well as my own." [19]

There were almost daily meetings, but Justice Jackson did not neglect the task of preparations: parallel with the negotiations in London the work of preparing the case was gathering momentum. The first weekend in July was seized by Jackson as an interval in the London talks to fly to Wiesbaden, to Frankfurt, to Nuremberg, to Salzburg, to Munich, and then to Paris, where he had set up an office in the Rue Presburg for processing a large collection of documents. He reported back to the London Conference:

I should like to raise a question and perhaps also suggest the answer of our Delegation. Lest there be some misunderstanding about it, I came here not only as a negotiator but also as a prosecutor with a staff prepared to stay here and, as soon as we finish the agreement to begin preparing the case. I have authority to sign any agreement which is within the general outlines of the document which we submitted at San Francisco and of the report I submitted to the President. I think it is important for our preparation of the case that we know how fast we can proceed. During the time the drafting committee was at work, I went to the Continent. I may report that we are having most satisfactory results from the examination of captured docu-

[19] *Ibid.*, Document XVIII.

ments. We are getting proof tracing the responsibility for these atrocities and war crimes back to the top authorities better than I ever expected we would get it. I did not think men would ever be so foolish as to put in writing some of the things the Germans did put in writing. The stupidity of it and the brutality of it would simply appall you. We want to go right ahead the day we agree here to start preparing for trial. I was wondering, first, whether the other conferees are authorized to sign as I am authorized to sign, or whether our work must be referred back to their governments; and second, whether they are authorized to proceed immediately with the preparation of the case as I am authorized to proceed with the preparation of the case.[20]

It was not clear what powers the Soviet representatives had been given or whether they would in fact be the prosecutors. Jackson warned again:

Some things that concern us all result from my discussions with General Clay last week on the Continent. We started with the idea, which you will find expressed in my report to the President (VIII), which the President accepted and approved, and which therefore constituted the official policy of the United States, that whether we got an agreement or not we would go ahead and try these people who are in our captivity. So we have been preparing for an international trial, but if we cannot agree on one we are going to dispose of these people on a record made in judicial fashion. Therefore, we have gone right ahead without waiting for an agreement.[21]

As the discussions went on three matters in particular gave rise to difficulty. Did the guilt of the accused have to be established by evidence before the Tribunal, or were they to be regarded as already guilty men, the Tribunal being concerned only with meting out what the Soviet representatives

[20] *Ibid.*, Document XXVII.   [21] *Ibid.*, Document XXVII.

called "justice." This was hardly a matter of subordinate importance but it was associated with another of even greater difficulty. The Soviet representatives were at last persuaded that the indictment should include a charge of waging a war of aggression. But they wanted to qualify or limit the charge to a "Hitlerite" war of aggression. Were they possibly thinking that any general definition of aggression might give rise to painful memories in the Baltic States? I do not know.

But, said General Nikitchenko:

The policy which has been carried out by the Axis powers has been defined as an aggressive policy in the various documents of the Allied nations and of all the United Nations, and the Tribunal would really not need to go into that.

Mr. Justice Jackson:

If we are to proceed on that basis, why do we need a trial at all?

General Nikitchenko:

The fact that the Nazi leaders are criminals has already been established. The task of the Tribunal is only to determine the measure of guilt of each particular person and mete out the necessary punishment—the sentence.[22]

Various compromises were suggested but Justice Jackson stood firm:

The draft before us submitted by the Soviet Delegation literally only confers jurisdiction to try persons; it does not, as I see it, define the substantive law which creates the crimes. Therefore, if this were adopted, it would be entirely open to the Tribunal if it thought the international law was such as to warrant it, to adjudge that, while these persons had committed the acts we charge, these acts were not crimes against inter-

[22] *Ibid.*, Document XXXVII.

national law and therefore to acquit them. That we think would make the trial a travesty.

Now let us take (a). If we look at it as defining a crime, it is one consisting of three elements: first, there must be "aggression against or domination over"; second, it must be carried out by Axis powers: it must be in violation of international law and treaties.

Then the second element contained in (a) is, it must be carried out by Axis powers. We would think that had no place in any definition because it makes an entirely partisan declaration of law. If certain acts in violation of treaties are crimes, they are crimes whether the United States does them or whether Germany does them, and we are not prepared to lay down a rule of criminal conduct against others which we would not be willing to have invoked against us. Therefore, we think the clause "carried out by the European Axis" so qualifies the statement that it deprives it of all standing and fairness as a juridical principle. Then the third element of (a), that all of this must be in violation of international law and treaties, brings us right back to the question which we set out to solve, which is to say that certain aggressions which have been declared illegal long before this war was begun are violations of international law, rather than to leave that to the Tribunal to argue about and possibly disagree about.[23]

Again, two or three days later:

That is one of the things we want to prove, because we want the Germans and anybody else to know that as far as the United States is concerned it regards any attack on the peace of the world as an international crime. It may become necessary to abandon the effort to try these people on that basis, but there are some things worse for me than failing to reach an agreement, and one of them is reaching an agreement which

23 *Ibid.*, Document XLIV.

would stultify the position which the United States has taken throughout.[24]

Again, Nikitchenko:

It is supposed then to condemn aggression or initiation of war in general or to condemn specifically aggressions started by the Nazis in this war? If the attempt is to have a general definition, that would not be agreeable.[25]

The other problem was where the Trial should take place. The Soviet representatives, for prestige or other reasons best known to them, wanted Berlin—and wanted indeed the whole proceeding to be very much under the aegis of the Control Commission. But while agreeing that the Control Commission might mitigate any sentences imposed, Justice Jackson was entirely unwilling that the Commission could review or in any way set aside the verdict and judgment. Berlin, moreover, was an entirely unsuitable place for a trial. It was a ruined city: there was no adequate Court House, no prison, none of the facilities needed. Nuremberg, which was of course a city of psychological significance to the Nazis, was in fact the only place in Germany where the necessary facilities remained. On the 18th of July, Jackson offered to lend his aircraft so that the representatives of the three other Powers could go there and see what was available: he invited them. All accepted. "We would be glad," said General Nikitchenko, "to take advantage of the kind invitation extended by Justice Jackson." Arrangements were made to fly off on the following Saturday. On Friday, the Soviet Delegation gave a lunch for the other delegations and said they could not go. Jackson offered to change the date to any other which was

24 *Ibid.*, Document LI.   25 *Ibid.*, Document LI.

convenient to them. No, they said—obviously on instructions from Moscow—they could not go. It was suggested that while the administrative seat of the Tribunal might be in Berlin, the first trial should be at Nuremberg. Mr. Sidney Alderman reported:

Professor Trainin would not agree to that. We tried "Headquarters," "Central Office," and various other formulae for the site at Berlin, but to no avail. He insisted on amending article 22 of the agreement so as to make it read that "There shall be established in Berlin an International Military Tribunal," et cetera. It became quite obvious in the discussion that he had it in mind that the Tribunal would be "permanently located" in Berlin, and its "archives" would be there, that preparations for trials would take place there, and, apparently, that the prisoners would be there.[26]

It was by now the 25th of July. Time was getting on. Even General Nikitchenko felt impelled to say that "if discussion went on he was afraid the war criminals would die of old age."

In the meantime, however, President Truman, Marshal Stalin, the Prime Minister Churchill, later to be replaced by Prime Minister Attlee, had arranged to meet in conference at Potsdam and the British had asked that the subject of the war criminals should be included on the agenda. Justice Jackson was apparently "rather appalled" at the idea that the Big Three might get involved in this very difficult and highly technical matter. But the British had been afraid that Russian suspicions of their own and the Americans intentions as to the trials might become an embarrassment, and they hoped to allay them. Justice Jackson flew to Potsdam and consulted with Mr. Secretary Byrnes on July

[26] *Ibid.*, Document XL.

26th. Eventually the subject was discussed both by the
Foreign Ministers and the Big Three. The Russians put
forward the proposal that the final communique of the
Conference should state that a Four Power Military Tribunal was to be established with power to try, condemn, and
execute the leading Nazis to be named by the Conference.
This greatly dismayed Justice Jackson: he felt that such a
decision by the Conference would confirm the Russians in
their intransigence about the definition of war crimes, the
seat of the Tribunal and so on. He told Judge Rosenman
that he almost despaired of reaching agreement with the
Russians and that the possibility of a Three Power Tribunal
without the Russians could not be excluded. He urged Judge
Rosenman so to inform the President. On August 1st, the
Big Three discussed the subject again: in the end a compromise was reached on the basis of a British proposal. The
three Governments reaffirmed their intention to bring the
war criminals to swift and sure justice, hoped that the London negotiations would lead to speedy agreement, and that
the trials would begin at the earliest possible date. The
first list of Defendants, they said, would be published on
September 1st.[27] There can be no doubt that Marshal
Stalin, reassured, then sent instructions to London that the
Soviet representatives must be more accommodating: the
change in Government in England also resulted in the
chairmanship of the London Conference being taken over
by Lord Chancellor Jowitt. He combined in high measure
the qualities of sauviter in modo with fortiter in re. Business
went through at the meeting on August 2nd with commendable expedition. The Russians did not persist in limit-
ing the crime of aggression to Nazi aggression but instead

[27] Conference of Berlin, 1945, Washington, 1960. Vol. II, p. 1489.

of the crime of war it was to be called the crime against peace. Similarly, agreement was reached about Nuremberg. Said General Nikitchenko:

We are prepared to agree to the first trial at Nuremberg, but we would like it considered that the administrative headquarters and the first meetings of the Tribunal and the prosecutors shall also take place in Berlin at a place to be designated by the Control Council. The first trial shall be held in Nuremberg and subsequent trials as we had it.[28]

All was, at last, set for formal documentation, and on August 8th the Agreement and Charter of the International Tribunal was duly signed. As Mr. Francis Biddle later wrote: "Robert Jackson's tireless energy and skill had finally brought the four nations together—a really extraordinary feat." [29] Thenceforward until the end of the Trial he succeeded in maintaining a remarkable degree of cooperation. Even before the Trial actually commenced, three other matters had to be disposed of, any one of which might have led to breakdown. The first of these involved the selection of the major criminals to be made defendants. The leaders at the Potsdam Conference had announced that the names of those to be tried would be published "within a month." There was not much time but in a sense the criminals chose themselves by the very notoriety of their conduct: it was not so much a question of whom to include but who could be left out. Originally, the American view had been that there should be fifty or sixty defendants. Jackson thought that apart from the obvious Nazi leaders, there

[28] International Conference on Military Tribunals, Document LIX.
[29] Francis Biddle, *In Brief Authority*, New York, 1962, p. 383.

should be brought to the first trial the top men in the various organizations and departments whose effort had contributed to the whole conspiracy and who, besides being individually and personally responsible for the crimes with which they were charged, would be in a sense representatives of the activities concerned. This presented difficulty only as to the industrialists. One of the obvious candidates was Schacht, who had never withheld his services as a brilliant financier from the Nazis and who was lucky to be acquitted. Another was Gustav Krupp, the senior member of the great German armament firm, which had made an enormous contribution to the Nazi war effort, and during the war had used slave labor. But Justice Jackson wished to include also Alfried Krupp and a number of other industrialists. Some of us felt that to have too many defendants, particularly of the same representative category, would detract from the impact of the trial, as one of the real ringleaders alone, and would bog it down in too much detail; in the end, Jackson was outvoted. As it later turned out, Gustav Krupp was too ill to be tried and Jackson then pressed for the substitution of Alfried. He was supported by the French and by the Russians, who would have been prepared to try anybody, guilty or not. I am afraid that I felt it necessary to oppose this motion, and I recall it as the only occasion on which I had any real difference of view with Jackson. To have included Alfried at the stage we had by then reached would have involved postponing the opening of the Trial, and I thought that this would have been a grave mistake. When the Motion came before the Tribunal, I added that the Trial was "not a game of football in which we could field a substitute." The Tribunal accepted this view and the Trial went on without any representative of Nazi industry in the dock, although Alfried was tried in later proceedings.

The other defendant whose trial gave rise to controversy was Rudolf Hess. In Jackson's words, he was ". . . . the engineer tending the party machinery, passing orders and propaganda down to the leadership corps, supervising every aspect of party activities and maintaining the organization as a loyal and ready instrument of power." The question was not whether he was guilty but whether he was sane. He flew to Britain in the middle of the war, landing in Scotland, and tried to make contact with the Duke of Hamilton in the apparent belief that with the assistance of the British aristocracy a peace might be negotiated. This was in itself some evidence of insanity! But the Russians had, and perhaps still have, extraordinary suspicions about it. Possibly they did not understand why we had not shot him out of hand; possibly they imagined we had actually negotiated for a separate peace, something it never occurred to us for one moment to do. At the Potsdam Conference, Stalin insisted that Hess must be tried as a war criminal, and we never dissented. Mr. Ernest Bevin, the Foreign Secretary, assured the Soviet Marshal that we would hand Hess over —and "send along a bill for his keep as well." But when the time came for Trial many thought that Hess was mentally unfit to stand trial, and his Counsel entered a plea to that effect. A panel of distinguished doctors examined him, and although considering him affected by amnesia and not normal in other respects, concluded that he was fit to stand his trial and Hess himself, in a very cogent and clear statement, asserted his right to be tried and his wish to stand beside his associates. The Tribunal so decided, but as the trial proceeded and we had an opportunity of observing his appearance and behavior, most of us felt doubtful. Mr. Justice Birkett recorded that in his final statement "Hess betrayed the signs of a disordered mind in almost every word he spoke." He was sentenced to imprisonment for life and he is still imprisoned, the solitary inmate of the Spandau prison. His continued imprisonment is a disgrace for which the Soviet Government alone is responsible. I do not believe that any civilized State now enforces imprisonment for life without mercy or remission. The other Allied Powers have urged that Hess be released. Only the Russians insist upon his continued incarceration.

The list of defendants decided, the next problem was settling the indictment itself, a document of 18,000 words. Once, however, the Russians had been persuaded that it was not only "Hitlerite" aggression but all wars of aggression which were to be indicted, no great difficulty arose until the last moment and, on the whole, Anglo-Saxon forms were followed. On one matter, however, there was disagreement. At one of the final meetings of the prosecuting counsel before the presentation of the indictment, the Russians insisted that it should include a charge that the Germans were guilty of the massacre of thousands of Polish officers whose bodies had been found, many shackled together and shot through the back of the head, in the Katyn Forest. Jackson opposed this. I asked Sir David Maxwell Fyfe, my Deputy, to examine the evidence and report to me on the merits. At that time he concluded that it was uncertain whether this horrible atrocity had been committed by the Russians or the Germans. I accordingly strongly supported Jackson and went privately to General Rudenko, the chief Russian prosecutor, to urge him, in the most tactful way, not to press the point. He insisted none the less, and rather than face a complete breakdown, the rest of us were forced to acquiesce. We informed General Rudenko explicitly, however, that we would ourselves not seek to establish this charge nor make any reference to it, and that the sole responsibility must rest upon the Soviet side of the prosecution. The evidence which the Russians eventually led upon the matter was inconclusive and the Tribunal completely ignored the whole charge. Whatever the truth about the Katyn massacre, none of the defendants at Nuremberg was in any way punished for it.

But even this acquiescence in their views did not enable the Russians at once to sign the indictment. The Judges and the chief prosecutors had gone to Berlin early in October, and the program was that the indictment would be formally and publicly presented to them there on October 15th. The day before, the Russians announced they could not sign it. They were evidently under instruction from Moscow, but what the difficulty was we never understood. They insisted upon postponement. We opposed their application but, in the end, the Tribunal, I think wisely, agreed to a three-day adjournment.

The final matter which, as it turned out, presented surprisingly little difficulty, was the selection of a President. The Charter had left this matter open. The Russians wished to have the Presidency rotated between the four Powers; the French had a nicely logical idea of a rotation by topics. Francis Biddle was an obvious choice. But during preliminary organizational meetings of the Tribunal in Berlin, the British Judge, Lord Justice Lawrence, possibly because he was the only one of the four who was still acting as a Judge in his own country, had somehow or other assumed the chair. Jackson, in a telegram he sent Biddle about a year later put the matter in this way:

It was generally known that representatives of all Nations were ready to agree upon the American member Francis Biddle as Presiding Officer. However, the United States was to be host to all the Nations at Nuremberg, had as its prisoners most of the defendants, had captured the bulk of the evidence and had been delegated a leading part in the prosecution. Under these conditions for the United States also to take the Presidency of the Tribunal would tend to make the trial too predominantly an American enterprise in the eyes of Europe and to relieve our associates powers of too much responsibility. Mr. Biddle in the interest of the United States declined the honour when it was clearly within his reach.[30]

This was true. General Nikitchenko, the Russian member, proposed Biddle, but Biddle and the French agreed to nominate Lawrence, and he was elected. As a matter of courtesy, however, Nikitchenko was asked to preside at the first meeting on October 18th in Berlin, to receive the indictment. And on October 18th according to the English *Times*, "with fitting dignity but workmanlike dispatch the Military Tribunal held its first open session." I lodged the indictment on behalf of the prosecuting powers, rules of procedure were laid down, and the opening of the Trial was fixed for a date thirty days after the service of the indictment upon the defendants.

The next day we went to Nuremberg. Much remained to be done. The American Army was reconstructing the court; apparatus was being put in for simultaneous translation, for telephone and telegraph facilities for the newspaper reporters who were to come in hundreds, accommodation and

[30] *Ibid.*, p. 386.

catering for all those concerned in the Trials—1,500 lunches were served in the court cafeteria each day—all this was being constructed and organized. But these were the domestic details, although Justice Jackson never lost sight of them. The major task was to be ready to open this greatest of all trials within a month, and here the burden lay more heavily upon Jackson than upon anyone else, for he was to open the case.

But we were ready. On November 20th, 1945, less than seven months after the surrender of Germany and of Justice Jackson's own appointment as Chief Prosecutor, in spite of all the deaths and disruptions, the difficulties and dislocations of the most terrible war the world had known, in spite of the manifold legal and technical problems involved, the Trial opened in solemn dignity and went on, day by day, in exorably to its end. As Jackson said in his opening address to the Tribunal:

In my country, established courts, following familiar procedures, applying well thumbed precedents and dealing with the legal consequences of local and limited events, seldom commence a trial within a year of the event in litigation. Yet less than eight months ago today the courtroom in which you sit was an enemy fortress in the hands of German S.S. troops. Less than eight months ago nearly all our witnesses and documents were in enemy hands. The law had not been codified, no procedures had been established, no tribunal was in existence, no usable courthouse stood here, none of the hundreds of tons of official German documents had been examined, no prosecuting staff had been assembled, nearly all of the present defendants were at large, and the four prosecuting powers had not yet joined in common cause to try them.[31]

[31] The Trial of German Major War Criminals, Part I, p. 50.

It was a remarkable achievement. And it was essentially an achievement dominated by the personality and dedication of Jackson himself. Statistically, the task can perhaps best be expressed in the succinct language of his own report to the President:

In preparation for the trial over 100,000 captured German documents were screened or examined and about 10,000 were selected for intensive examination as having probable evidentiary value. Of these, about 4,000 were translated into four languages and used, in whole or in part, in the trial as exhibits. Millions of feet of captured moving picture film were examined and over 100,000 feet brought to Nuremberg. Relevant sections were prepared and introduced as exhibits. Over 25,000 captured still photographs were brought to Nuremberg, together with Hitler's personal photographer who took most of them. More than 1,800 were selected and prepared for use as exhibits.[32]

And then the trial itself:

It occupied 216 days of trial time. Thirty-three witnesses were called and examined for the prosecution. Sixty-one witnesses and 19 defendants testified for the defense; 143 additional witnesses gave testimony by interrogatories for the defense. The proceedings were conducted and recorded in four languages—English, German, French, and Russian—and daily transcripts in the language of his choice was provided for each prosecuting staff and all counsel for defendants. The English transcript of the proceedings covers over 17,000 pages. All proceedings were sound-reported in the original language used.[33]

Over 30,000 photostats, fifty-million pages of typed matter, and more than 4,000 recorded disks were produced.

Of the actual trial much has been written and said (al-

---

[32] International Conference on Military Tribunals, Document LXIII.
[33] *Ibid.*, Document LXIII.

though never before by me) and I shall say little now. Great organizational problems naturally still continued. Regularly each week, and often more frequently, meetings of the Chief Prosecutors were held to resolve these and discuss and coordinate procedure. Over these Jackson presided. It was arranged between the Chief Prosecutors that while all should be at liberty to cover any part of the indictment, each would assume the main responsibility for presenting a particular part of the case. Jackson's responsibility was especially for the first and basic count of the indictment —the conspiracy to wage aggressive war. He built up an overwhelming case, based almost entirely on captured German documents, but welded together in a speech of great power. It was, for such an occasion, by no means a long speech. I wish I could quote more of it. Let me remind you of one of the opening passages:

In the prisoners' dock sit twenty-odd broken men. Reproached by the humiliation of those they have led, almost as bitterly as by the desolation of those they have attacked, their personal capacity for evil is forever past. It is hard now to perceive in these miserable men as captives the power by which as Nazi leaders they once dominated much of the world and terrified most of it. Merely as individuals their fate is of little consequence to the world.

What makes this inquest significant is that these prisoners represent sinister influences that will lurk in the world long after their bodies have returned to dust. We will show them to be living symbols of racial hatreds, of terrorism and violence, and of the arrogance and cruelty of power. They are symbols of fierce nationalisms and of militarism, of intrigue and warmaking which have embroiled Europe generation after generation, crushing its manhood, destroying its homes, and impoverishing its life. They have so identified themselves with the philosophies they conceived, and with the forces they have directed, that any tenderness to them is a victory and an encouragement to all the evils which are attached to their names. Civilization can afford no compromise with the social forces which would gain renewed strength if we deal ambiguously or indecisively with the men in whom those forces now precariously survive.

What these men stand for we will patiently and temperately disclose.[34]

In these passages he came to deal with the legal basis of the proceedings:

It is true, of course, that we have no judicial precedent for this Charter. But International Law is more than a scholarly collection of abstract and immovable principles. It is an outgrowth of treaties and agreements between nations and accepted customs. Yet every custom has its origin in some single act and every agreement has to be initiated by the action of some State. Unless we are prepared to abandon every principle of growth in International Law we cannot deny that our own day has the right to institute customs and conclude agreements that will themselves become sources of a newer and strengthened International Law. International Law is not capable of development by the normal processes of legislation for there is no continuing international legislative authority. Innovations and revisions in International Law are brought about by the actions of governments such as those I have cited, designed to meet a change in circumstances. It grows as did the Common Law. A few decisions reached from time to time in adapting legal principles to new situations. The fact is that when the law evolved by the case method as did the Common Law, and the International Law must do if it is to advance at all, it does advance at the expense of those who wrongly guessed the law

[34] The Trial of German Major War Criminals, Part I, pp. 49–50.

and learned too late their error. The law so far as International Law can be decreed, had been clearly announced when these acts took place.[35]

These passages are from the peroration of his opening speech:

I am too well aware of the weakness of juridical action alone to contend that in itself your decision under this Charter can prevent future wars. Judicial action always comes after the event. Wars are started only on the theory and in the confidence that they can be won. Personal punishment to be suffered only in event the war is lost will probably not be a sufficient deterrent to prevent a war while the warmakers feel the chances of defeat to be negligible. But the ultimate steps in avoiding periodic wars which are inevitable in a system of international lawlessness, is to make statesmen responsible to law. And let me make clear that while this law is first applied against German aggressors, the law includes, and if it is to serve a useful purpose, it must condemn aggression by any other nations including those which sit here now in judgment. We are able to do away with domestic tyranny and violence and aggression by those in power against the rights of their own people only when we make all men answerable to law. This, however, presents mankind's desperate effort to apply the discipline of the law to statesmen who have used their powers of state to attack the foundations of the world's peace and to commit aggressions against the rights of their neighbors.[36]

Civilization asks whether law is so laggard as to be utterly helpless to deal with crimes of this magnitude by criminals of this order of importance. It does not expect that you can make war impossible. It does expect that your juridical action will put the forces of International Law, its precepts, its prohibitions and, most of all, its sanctions, on the side of peace, so that men

35 *Ibid.*   36 *Ibid.*

and women of good will, in all countries, may have "leave to live by no man's leave, underneath the law." [37]

None of the arts of the actor are here. This is no dramatic declamation, but calmly in words of dignity and authority the demand of a lawyer and statesman too that law and justice should in the end prevail.

The trial proceeded on its allotted course. There were regular meetings of the Chief Prosecutors. It would be idle to pretend that there were never difficulties, never vexatious incidents. But that they were overcome was largely due to the great respect and friendship which we all developed for Jackson, upon whom the main responsibility fell, primus inter pares with the Chief Prosecutors of the other countries. It would be idle, too, to pretend that there were no criticisms. Jackson was not immune from the human frailties we all possess. Sometimes he was impatient, occasionally he was irritable. Birkett thought he was inclined to be pompous or even vain. But these were criticisms which were laid at times against us all. Indeed, there were singularly few personal difficulties, and such as there were, for the most part, quickly overcome. But about one matter I should perhaps make some comment, for it has been given prominence in many books. I refer to Justice Jackson's cross-examination of Goering. It was not a success. And that this was so was due, I think, to a combination of factors. Goering himself was a most remarkable man. A criminal no doubt. But a courageous one, a man of great ability and of outstanding personality. One felt of him that in some respects his personality could dominate the whole proceedings if he sought to make it so. Indeed, Mr. Justice Birkett put it higher:

[37] *Ibid.*, Part I, p. 85.

Throughout this trial the dead Hitler has been present at every session. . . . But Goering is the man who has dominated the proceedings and that, remarkably enough, without ever uttering a word. . . . That in itself is a very remarkable achievement and illuminates much that was obscure in the history of the last few years.[38]

It was curious that he asserted himself so little. But during his cross-examination his ability was left in no doubt. Nor his agility. This was a man to be cross-examined in one way only—by following that first axiom of cross-examination in a criminal trial, which is never to ask a question without knowing that there is only one inescapable answer to be given to it—usually a "yes" or a "no," and by that process to lead the witness up to the last fatal but inescapable response. Jackson would have been the last to pretend that he was an expert in this art: he had definite scruples about a criminal practice: "I wouldn't want to cultivate a criminal practice. . . . Pretty soon it is a hard thing to know which is the criminal and which the counsel." [39] His forte was, rather, advocacy and argument. I did not myself hear his cross-examination, but one of the members of the British team, the present Attorney-General of England, Sir Elwyn Jones, Q.C., of whom Mr. Biddle wrote, "He was always relevant and lucid and of great assistance to the Tribunal. . . . It was the best presentation we have yet heard," has recently written to me:

From my recollection of his cross-examination of Goering, Bob's error was to regard his confrontation with Goering as one between the personification of Nazi tyranny on the one hand and the quintessence of liberal democracy on the other—which

[38] Montgomery Hyde, *Norman Birkett*, London, 1964, p. 510.
[39] Eugene H. Gerhart, *Robert Jackson, America's Advocate*, p. 43.

of course in one way it was. This let him into a difficult cross-examination field where opinions were challenged instead of facts, always an unrewarding exercise.

In a sense Jackson's lack of success was due to his intellectual honesty. His whole case was to expose the evil philosophies with which the Nazis had sought to dominate the world: this inevitably involved him in putting matters of opinion and in an argumentative rather than a factual exchange. But a third factor in the failure was perhaps a weakness of the Tribunal in allowing excess latitude to Goering, and Jackson protested against this in vain. As to this, Birkett recorded in his diary:

But perhaps the most important factor of all was the failure of the Tribunal to intervene when the situation developed and to retain control of the proceedings. Goering was allowed to make long statements in reply to almost every question and with his combination of knowledge and ability he was able to present at least a plausible case on almost every aspect of the matter.[40]

Birkett urged that the Tribunal should assert its authority and limit Goering to answering questions and not making speeches, but this the Tribunal did not do. In the result, Jackson's cross-examination did not demolish Goering. Faced by this situation the British team, in the words of one of its members "spent the night digging up documents signed by Goering personally showing him to be a friend of Himmler, a bandit and a thug." The result was by contrast an effective cross-examination by which Sir David Maxwell Fyfe made his reputation. But Fyfe was, of course, essentially a criminal lawyer who had learnt how to cross-

[40] Montgomery Hyde, *Norman Birkett*, p. 511.

examine from the Magistrates Courts up, and who would not normally engage in philosophical exercises. Even so, the cross-examination did not satisfy Birkett's high standard. On May 1st he wrote in his Diary:

Despite the flattering press notices of the cross-examination by the British it remains true that a true cross-examination has not yet been given. It is a cross-examination in name only which consists in putting incriminating documents to the witness. The true art of cross-examination is something in a different plane altogether and it has not yet been seen at Nuremberg in any shape or form.[41]

It must be added that there are critical passages in Birkett's Diaries about many of those engaged in the Trial. Birkett was a man to whom I owe a great deal: a veritable guide, philosopher, and friend. He was also one of our greatest advocates. But at this period he was a disappointed and frustrated man. As his biographer says, he was very conscious of his subordinate role as an alternate judge. He had recorded "a secret anguish" that he had not been appointed, as he had at first been asked, to be the senior British Judge, and not long after Nuremberg he was "feeling personally depressed and dispirited." I think that some of his impatient comments on the Nuremberg proceeding were due to these considerations.

None of them can detract from Justice Jackson's major achievement there, which was not the success or failure of any single intervention, but the success of the trial as a whole. Sir Elwyn Jones paid this tribute:

Jackson was of course the real driving force that by sheer energy and will got Nuremberg under way. We know he was difficult

41 *Ibid.*, p. 500.

at times. But in my view his two main Nuremberg speeches are amongst the finest ever pronounced in any Court for the great beauty of their language and the passionate conviction they expressed.

As for the "difficulties at times," another member of the British team, now an English Judge, has written:

One of the very nice things about Jackson was his friendliness to all the lesser lights such as myself and the other junior members of the British delegation. He was always approachable and ready to help if he could.

And so I come to Jackson's great final summing up. In those far-off days we were most of us still a little starry-eyed —still hoping that cooperation between the Great Powers would lead the world forward in peace. But Jackson's warning was plain:

It is common to think of our own time as standing at the apex of civilization, from which the deficiencies of preceding ages may patronizingly be viewed in the light of what is assumed to be "progress." The reality is that in the long perspective of history the present century will not hold an admirable position, unless its second half is to redeem its first. These two-score years in this twentieth century will be recorded in the book of years as some of the most bloody in all annals. Two world wars have left a legacy of dead which number more than all the armies engaged in any war that made ancient or medieval history. No half-century ever witnessed slaughter on such a scale, such cruelties and inhumanities, such wholesale deportations of peoples into slavery, such annihilations of minorities. The terror of Torquemada pales before the Nazi Inquisition. These deeds are the overshadowing historical facts by which generations to come will remember this decade. If we cannot eliminate the causes and prevent the repetition of these barbaric events, it is not an irresponsible prophecy to say that this twentieth century may yet succeed in bringing the doom of civilization.[42]

Leaving it to the experts to comb the evidence and write volumes on their specialities, Jackson pictured in broad strokes the offenses whose acceptance as lawful would threaten the continuity of civilization. "I must", as Kipling put it "splash at a ten-league canvas with brushes of camel's hair." It was not a long speech. It was a speech illuminated by humanity, clearly and vividly illustrating the crimes that had been committed, the rule of law which was to be vindicated. It was a speech that no one who heard it will forget: a speech which future historians and statesmen would do well to remember.

Counsel for many of the defendants seek to dismiss the charge of a common plan or conspiracy on the ground that the pattern of the Nazi plan does not fit into the concept of conspiracy applicable in German law to the plotting of a highway robbery or a burglary. Their concept of conspiracy is in the terms of a stealthy meeting in the dead of night, in a secluded hideout, in which a group of felons plot every detail of a specific crime. The Charter forestalls resort to such parochial and narrow concepts of conspiracy taken from local law by using the additional and non-technical term, "common plan." Omitting entirely the alternative term of "conspiracy," the Charter reads that "leaders, organizers, instigators, and accomplices participating in the formulation or execution of a common plan to commit" any of the described crimes, "are responsible for all acts performed by any persons in execution of such plan."

The Charter concept of a common plan really represents the conspiracy principle in an international context. A common

---

[42] The Trial of German Major War Criminals, Part 19, p. 382.

plan or conspiracy to seize the machinery of a State, to commit crimes against the peace of the world, to blot a race out of existence, to enslave millions, and to subjugate and loot whole nations cannot be thought of in the same terms as the plotting of petty crimes, although the same underlying principles are applicable. Little gangsters may plan who will carry a pistol and who a stiletto, who will approach a victim from the front and who from behind, and where they will waylay him. But in planning a war, the pistol becomes a Wehrmacht, the stiletto a Luftwaffe. Where to strike is not a choice of dark alleys, but a matter of world geography. The operation involves the manipulation of public opinion, the law of the State, the police power, industry, and finance. The baits and bluffs must be translated into a nation's foreign policy. Likewise, the degree of stealth which points to a guilty purpose in a conspiracy will depend upon its object. The clandestine preparations of a State against international society, although camouflaged to those abroad, might be quite open and notorious among its own people. But stealth is not an essential ingredient of such planning. Parts of the common plan may be proclaimed from the housetops, as anti-Semitism was, and parts of it kept under cover, as rearmament for a long time was. It is a matter of strategy how much of the preparation shall be made public, as was Goering's announcement in 1935 of the creation of an air force, and how much shall be kept covert, as in the case of the Nazis' use of shovels to teach "labor corps" the manual of arms. The forms of this grand type of conspiracy are amorphous, the means are opportunistic, and neither can divert the law from getting at the substance of things.[43]

It is of interest perhaps to recall his summary of the case against one who was acquitted, utterly damning as we thought his summation was at that time:

[43] *Ibid.*, pp. 397–98.

Nearly all the defendants take two or more conflicting positions. Let us illustrate the inconsistencies of their positions by the record of one defendant—who, if pressed, would himself concede that he is the most intelligent, honorable and innocent man in the dock. That is Schacht. And this is the effect of his own testimony—but let us not forget that I recite it not against him alone, but because most of its self-contradictions are found in the testimony of several defendants.

Schacht did not openly join the Nazi movement until it had won, nor openly desert it until it had lost. He admits that he never gave it public opposition, but asserts that he never gave it private loyalty. When we demand of him why he did not stop the criminal course of the regime in which he was a Minister, he says he had not a bit of influence. When we ask why he remained a member of the criminal regime, he tells us that by sticking on he expected to moderate its program. Like a Brahmin among Untouchables, he could not bear to mingle with the Nazis socially, but never could he afford to separate from them politically. Of all the Nazi aggressions by which he now claims to have been shocked there is not one that he did not support before the world with the weight of his name and prestige. Having armed Hitler to blackmail a continent, his answer now is to blame England and France for yielding.

Schacht always fought for his position in a regime he now affects to despise. He sometimes disagreed with his Nazi confederates about what was expedient in reaching their goal, but he never dissented from the goal itself. When he did break with them in the twilight of the regime, it was over tactics, not principles. From then on he never ceased to urge others to risk their positions and their necks to forward his plots, but never on any occasion did he hazard either of his own. He now boasts that he personally would have shot Hitler if he had had the opportunity, but the German newsreel shows that even after the fall of France, when he faced the living Hitler, he stepped out of line to grasp the hand he now claims to loathe and hung upon the words of the man he now says he thought unworthy of belief. Schacht says he steadily "sabotaged" the Hitler Government. Yet the most relentless secret service in the world never detected him doing the regime any harm until long after he knew the war to be lost and the Nazis doomed. Schacht, who dealt in "hedges" all his life, always kept himself in a position to claim that he was in either camp. The plea for him is as specious on analysis as it is persuasive on first sight. Schacht represents the most dangerous and reprehensible type of opportunism—that of the man of influential position who is ready to join a movement that he knows to be wrong because he thinks it is winning.[44]

And then, after examining other cases, his final words ring in my memory still:

It is against such a background that these defendants now ask this Tribunal to say that they are not guilty of planning, executing, or conspiring to commit this long list of crimes and wrongs. They stand before the record of this trial as blood-stained Gloucester stood by the body of his slain King. He begged of the widow, as they beg of you: "Say I slew them not." And the Queen replied: "Then say they were not slain. But dead they are. . . ." If you were to say of these men that they are not guilty, it would be as true to say that there has been no war, that there are no slain, that there has been no crime.[45]

And so this great Assize drew to its close.

One asks today whether it was all worthwhile. What did Jackson and the rest of us who walked with him achieve? Was the law vindicated, was peace made more secure? Jackson himself, in his final report to the President, gave a balanced account which I repeat here in part:

[44] *Ibid.*, p. 403.   [45] *Ibid.*, p. 406.

Of course, it would be extravagant to claim that agreements or trials of this character can make aggressive war or persecution of minorities impossible, just as it would be extravagant to claim that our federal laws make federal crime impossible. But we cannot doubt that they strengthen the bulwarks of peace and tolerance. The four nations through their prosecutors and through their representatives on the Tribunal, have enunciated standards of conduct which bring new hope to men of good will and from which future statesmen will not lightly depart. These standards by which the Germans have been condemned will become the condemnation of any nation that is faithless to them.

By the Agreement and this trial we have put International Law squarely on the side of peace as against aggressive warfare, and on the side of humanity as against persecution. In the present depressing world outlook it is possible that the Nuremberg trial may constitute the most important moral advance to grow out of this war. The trial and decision by which the four nations have forfeited the lives of some of the most powerful political and military leaders of Germany because they have violated fundamental International Law, does more than anything in our time to give to International Law what Woodrow Wilson described as "the kind of vitality it can only have if it is a real expression of our moral judgment." [46]

On December 11, 1946, the General Assembly unanimously adopted resolution 95(I), which, inter alia, affirmed "the principles of international law recognised by the Charter of the Nuremberg Tribunal and the judgment of the Tribunal." By a resolution of the following year (177(II) of November 21, 1947) the General Assembly directed the International Law Commission to formulate the principles of international law recognised in the Tribunals'

---

[46] Conference on Military Trials, Document LXIII.

Charter and in its judgment. Subsequently, this exercise and the related one of preparing a draft code of offenses against the peace and security of mankind became tied up with the question of defining aggression, and no further United Nations action has been taken on the formulation of the Nuremberg principles.

Looking back now, over twenty years later at a world still torn with lawlessness and war, I cannot pretend that the trial has so far had that effect on the course of history for which we had hoped. It is a matter of bitter disappointment, indeed of shame, in which perhaps we all must share.

At the Trial itself we had a close and warm relationship with our Russian colleagues. We thought we knew them intimately and could regard them as friends. But when the Trial was over and we went our respective ways, we became, in spite of many attempts to communicate, completely cut off from them. This apparent veto by the Communist regime upon ordinary human relationships between individuals is one of its great inhumanities. In recent years, however, I am glad to say, Mr. Volchkov, the Soviet alternate Judge, has made several friendly calls in England, so perhaps some day we can hope for a change. What is more frightening are the cynical violations which have since occurred of the rules of International Law as restated at Nuremberg and solemnly adopted thereafter by the United Nations. Korea, Hungary, Kashmir, Algeria, the Congo, Vietnam. Our hopes at Nuremberg have certainly been so far unfulfilled. But it does not follow that Nuremberg was in vain. In all our countries we have laws against murder and robbery: men are condemned for committing these crimes. And yet these crimes continue and even multiply. Is this a criticism of the laws which forbid them? It is not. It is a criticism of man's weakness in enforcing them or his wickedness in disregarding them. The Nuremberg judgment still stands as a clear statement of the law of Nations. If in the end mankind is to survive at all its principles must prevail.

Let me, as a final personal tribute to the brave idealist who did so much to enable that statement of the law of Nations to be so clearly made, quote again from a letter from the present Attorney-General of England:

My last memory of Bob is of lunching in his room at the Supreme Court with Felix Frankfurter during the height of the McCarthy horror. There were the four flags from the Nuremberg Court room behind Bob's desk with the Hammer and Sickle of the Soviet flag unashamedly exposed.

It is so, too, that I like to remember him.

                                        LORD SHAWCROSS